W9-AEO-795

LIBRARY

FD
31
H187
1994
c.2

ASOC
LIBRARY

MANAGEMENT OF QUALITY

QUALITY

STRATEGIES TO IMPROVE QUALITY AND THE BOTTOM LINE

MANAGEMENT OF QUALITY

STRATEGIES TO IMPROVE QUALITY AND THE BOTTOM LINE

Jack Hagan

ASQC Quality Press
Milwaukee, Wisconsin

BUSINESS ONE IRWIN
Burr Ridge, Illinois
New York, New York

©1994 by ASQC

All rights reserved. No part of this book may be
reproduced in any form or by any means electronic, mechanical,
photocopying, recording, or otherwise, without the prior
written permission of the publishers.

*From a Declaration of Principals jointly adopted by a Committee
of the American Bar Association and a Committee of Publishers.*

Sponsoring editor: Jean Marie Geracie
Project editor: Karen M. Smith
Production manager: Laurie Kersch
Designer: Larry J. Cope
Art coordinator: Heather Burbridge
Art Studio: Monotype Composition
Compositor: Precision Typographers
Typeface: 10.5/12 Times Roman
Printer: Book Press, Inc.

ASQC Quality Press:
  Marketing administrator: Mark Olson
  Acquisitions editor: Susan Westergard
  Production editor: Annette Wall

Library of Congress Cataloging-in-Publication Data

Hagan, Jack.
    Management of quality: strategies to improve quality and the
bottom line / Jack Hagan.
        p.   cm.
    Includes bibliographical references and index.
    ISBN 1-55623-924-6
    1. Industrial management.   2. Quality control.   I. Title.
HD31.H187   1994
658.5³⁄₄62—dc20   93–9817

Printed in the United States of America
1 2 3 4 5 6 7 8 9 0 BP 0 9 8 7 6 5 4 3

ASQC
Quality Press
611 East Wisconsin Avenue
Milwaukee, WI 53202

PREFACE

The failures of American management systems have reached epic proportions—if you believe only half of what is recounted in the newspapers and business journals. The reason most often offered is a failure to *listen to the customer* and a failure to appreciate and adopt the principles of quality improvement. To support this thesis, most key business functions, when examined in detail as an integral part of companywide quality improvement, prove to be relatively unknown quantities in terms of their actual net profit value. Most pronounced in this discovery is the great potential for performance improvement that generally exists.

Among the many explanations for this surprising paradox of value is that most quality improvement campaigns have stemmed from the immediate pressures of competition rather than from the realized needs of American business enterprises. Quality improvement's development and profitable use have therefore been somewhat independent of any natural business growth pattern; hence the competitive potential of this stepchild of industry has hardly been touched.

Serious attempts at making quality improvement a respected and useful part of all company functions are often frustrated by simple misunderstandings of intent and value. In many such situations, the role of quality improvement has become one of appeasing the customer—and of *fooling yourself and your company*. While this balancing act can easily become an interesting and challenging undertaking in itself, the usefulness of such activity is limited. Sooner or later, specific customer demands overlap the ability to make a profit, and trouble is unavoidable. Many company managers have seen this kind of trouble firsthand. Some have survived; others have moved on to other endeavors.

The intent of this book is to examine in detail the inherent business value of every feature of quality improvement—in an attempt to prove that "quality does not cost, it pays." As such, it deals with fundamental, business-oriented objectives for each quality improvement task and with the unintended but deeply ingrained obstacles that are generally encountered in working toward those objectives. It is not a manual of techniques. More than adequate material is already available on ways to resolve almost every conceivable quality problem. What is lacking in most of the literature, however, is the kind of detailed, practical information that will attract management understanding, support, and leadership for conversion to a *quality-first* organization.

This book is management oriented. Executive management, general management, staff management, associate management, functional management, and quality improvement management—all need the same understanding of quality improvement and its basic profit-oriented objectives. After more than 30 years in the quality management business, I am firmly convinced that the most serious problems of industry are rooted in the difficulties inherent in communication between industry's management and its workers and customers—a communication that seriously lacks integrity and thereby *prevents* people from ever pulling together for the same, shared goals.

When individual company managements are up against really tough competition, as most U.S. companies today find themselves, they tend to look for helpful changes almost everywhere else (e.g., economic policy, mandated regulations, tax structure, trade policy) except their own knowledge of what really makes a company competitive. They question everything except their own theories of management. This book will highlight that point.

The book starts by exploring the nature of quality management today and showing it to be in a state of transition—various stages of concern, action, and progress. It goes on to describe and explain the ultimate plateau of business activity that serves to model, for all companies and businesses, the desired quality management of tomorrow—their *prescription for survival*. It probes the deepest meanings of this prescription and provides ideas and guidance for planning, implementing, and sustaining an effective quality crusade. This is presented within a framework of management understanding and conduct—that is, in a management perspective rather than the "how-to" details, which are readily available in abundance. It does not deal with what makes managers and leaders act—only with how they *must* act. As such, it is like a map showing both the required destination and the ways to get there.

Some of the key points of the book's message are presented in more than one place, but always from a different perspective. Each section is presented as a total entity—that is, in a way that will *stand alone* for those readers to whom it may have special appeal. Each succeeding section, however, flows with the theme of the book.

Overall, this book will provide sufficient perspective and understanding of the *business of quality* to initiate and foster honest and productive communications. It will—hopefully—promote giant steps forward in America's quest for the fruits of quality improvement. If, as a result, American mangements better evaluate their quality position and then act on the genuine business opportunities presented by *quality improvement*, the book's purpose will have been achieved.

Jack Hagan

ACKNOWLEDGMENTS

I am deeply grateful to many individuals and organizations who provided substantial knowledge, experience, and assistance in the general pursuit of this project. Without their contributions, there would be no book. My sincere personal thanks go to the following.

My good friend and colleague, Frank Scanlon, prodded and helped me to *think things out*; the ITT Corporation gave me the opportunity to *experience quality improvement*; the U.S. Department of Defense shared their pioneering work in total quality management (TQM); and I learned much from all of my professional associates in the American Society for Quality Control.

Special thanks are due to the publishers for providing me with a unique opportunity to further develop and expand my thoughts on the subject of *quality management*.

Above all, I wish to thank my wife, Ruth, for her encouragement and moral support throughout the many months and the numerous struggles that made up the total effort.

J. H.

CONTENTS

PART 2
QUALITY MANAGEMENT TOMORROW:
THE IDEAL MANAGEMENT SYSTEM

INTRODUCTION

Most businesses have acknowledged the basic need for quality improvement, as evidenced by a myriad of quality improvement activities. In response to the relentless growth of competitive pressures, manufacturing companies have confronted the realities of worldwide quality competition; and in turn, they have achieved important advances in the technology and results of product quality control.

Concurrently, more and more service companies are establishing quality improvement programs of their own. Altogether, there has been an explosion of new control tools and improvement techniques developed and brought into play. And companies by the score are realizing that the management of quality is a critical companywide endeavor, driven by the growing and acknowledged power of the customer.

This "quality revolution" in America now clearly encompasses the broadest possible spectrum of companies engaged in international commerce—as well as all internal company functions and operations. For product manufacturing companies, managing product quality is not enough. Managing the quality performance of all administrative, planning, and product support areas is the new competitive strategy. Companies engaged in service business are encountering the same forces of quality-driven competition that have been and continue to confront manufacturing companies in the world marketplace.

The service sector has unquestionably become the new foundation of strength and business opportunity for American industry. As the main engine for economic growth, the service sector faces the same stiff competition as the manufacturing sector. The term *service industries* comprises a broad and still-growing spectrum of businesses, limited only by the imagination of America's newest entrepreneurs. It includes banking, insurance, financial service, real estate, food service, hospitality, publishing, printing, logistics, entertainment, broadcasting, retailing, leasing, distribution, laboratory service, health care, repair service, construction, education, research, transportation, utilities, government, communications, data processing, and other business services.

Historically, while manufacturing companies were being constantly bombarded with the need for quality improvement, the service sector began to discover some of the quality movement's inherent opportunities for business improvement. Publicized quality successes of manufacturing companies, coupled with the continued advance of service business competition, contributed heavily to the present concern for quality improvement within service sector businesses. In response to this concern, large numbers of service companies are currently engaged in some form of quality program or system.

The American version of quality improvement has slowly but surely evolved into a movement of monumental proportions—symbolized by a still-growing number of consultants, conferences, educational programs, books, and other promotional materials. The thrust of the effort seems to favor improvement concepts that involve the entire company—people, processes, and business strategies—over methodology alone. Another sign of the times is the emergence of more quality professionals into high-level company positions who can provide the knowledge and grass roots leadership many companies so desperately need.

Despite the multitude of different quality programs being discussed and started in all industries, a clear majority of business executives today remain personally uncommitted—or they do not fully understand and truly support what they are committed to. They may accept the idea that quality has to become an integral part of each company operation but fail to realize this means to be in a constant state of conversion from today's level of quality management toward the ultimate that can and must be achieved. Part of their subconscious rejection of the obvious is related to an inherent unwillingness to accept that *genuine quality progress means being completely open to change in the way the business is conceived and managed.*

As a result of this widespread lack of complete understanding and the fear of wholehearted commitment, quality has not yet fully arrived for U.S. businesses. Executives must still be sold on and convinced of its value, despite years of evidence of its positive impact on the economic successes of most major Japanese companies. To combat this crisis, U.S. industry must make quality improvement a major business effort of its own.

Unfortunately, the immense variety of quality improvement help available has made it too easy for managements to reach out for particular aspects of quality improvement—such as statistical process control, structured problem solving, employee participation programs, team concepts and so forth—without ever taking the time to understand the big picture. If all the organizations that claim to be engaged in quality improvement, as promoted by its advocates, were in fact doing so, the rest of the industrial world would be screaming for mercy. That, of course, is not happening—but *it could happen* if quality improvement were studied and understood as an integrated business entity. That's the picture, or vision, this book will attempt to portray.

PART 1

QUALITY MANAGEMENT TODAY IN A STATE OF TRANSITION

CHAPTER 1

THE TREND TOWARD COMPANYWIDE QUALITY SYSTEMS[1]

The decade of the 1980s saw many breakthroughs in quality management that laid the foundation for the complete integration of quality into American business operations. An American Society for Quality Control (ASQC) Gallup survey[2] confirms significant movement in this direction, while still identifying opportunities and needs for further progress, especially at that "critical juncture where good intentions face off against the realities of the hard work involved in the achievement of quality improvement." American industries must place more emphasis on extensive employee education and the important role of people— as compared to operating equipment and methodologies. Service quality, for both product and service companies, received the highest rating among a list of critical issues facing American companies in the nineties.

Some of America's most prominent quality experts[3] support the idea that remarkable changes occurred in the eighties, including:

- An increase in the overall awareness of the business value of quality improvement across all industries.
- A growth in the important contributions of the quality professional.

According to the experts, the eighties saw a complete revolution in the quality improvement business. People started to believe that quality improvement applies to every segment of the organization and is a powerful tool for cultural change, rather than the other way around. The experts also note the dramatic and positive results of quality improvement, such as:

- A more complete understanding of the customer.
- Spontaneous teamwork throughout the company.
- A massive rediscovery of the importance of the process.

The real source of these positive results—and the key trend of the 1980s—was the introduction and widely growing acceptance of companywide quality improvement (CWQI) programs by a broad spectrum of companies and businesses. In general, this concept promotes participation by all departments and all members of an organization in the quality improvement of every work process, directly and indirectly. More specifically, it provides a transition of ideas to bring widening attention to companywide opportunities for performance improvement. As you might expect, however, different approaches, different levels of commitment, and different degrees of involvement all led to a variety of results.

Let's now explore the nature of this trend.

THE CHALLENGE

Response to market pressures for overall quality improvement has been different for manufacturing companies than for companies in the service sector. Following the initial impact of worldwide product quality competition, led by the Japanese, the manufacturing sector has been in an uphill struggle for survival. Some of the hardest hit of these companies, however, have provided leadership for the great American comeback, forging the way for America's competitive reentry into the world marketplace for products.

Before continuing with the American story, and to emphasize the urgent need for continued forward progress, it is important to note that the Japanese have not been standing still during the eighties.[4] They have taken quality improvement technology into a stage that deploys the "voice of the customer" throughout the entire company—mobilizing all employees to concentrate on continued quality improvement at lower costs.

The Japanese consider quality, by definition, to affect the cost of design; efficiencies in manufacturing, assembly, sales, service, and customer ownership; and the overall value of the product to society. As they see it, the achievement of quality means controlling the quality of management, the quality of human behavior, the quality of individual performance, the quality of the work environment, the quality of product, and the quality of customer service. As you can see, their quality goals are clear and total.

Meanwhile, getting back to the general trend of U.S. manufacturing companies, most have some pattern of *product quality control*, for which there are many excellent programs available.[5] These well-known, basic quality control programs—created in America many years ago but not fully appreciated by U.S. companies until modern Japanese companies proved their value—deal primarily with the application of statistical controls to the product definition and manufacturing processes. They do not greatly concern functions other than those directly involved in the outgoing quality levels of delivered products.

For these product-oriented companies, the introduction of companywide quality improvement opens the door for the first time to staff functions like marketing, accounting, and design engineering to get involved in the quality improvement of their basic professional work. These departments and all other administrative and support areas of the manufacturing business are at the heart of where the most significant improvement has to take place if the company is to become truly competitive in today's marketplace. But this attempt to involve professional personnel in the quality improvement process has not occurred without some unique challenges.

Many members and managers of staff areas being invited to join a quality crusade are finding that they must drastically change how they view their jobs and departments. In effect, they are being challenged to contribute more directly to the bottom line. Some functions may actually be challenged by outside entrepreneurial businesses offering competitive services at discount prices.

In short, staff support areas are being asked to run leaner and to justify the value versus cost of their services. This is daringly new for staff professionals not accustomed to having their highly qualified, company-unique work output critically observed and challenged. Rather, they are more accustomed to having their professional competence accepted at face value—having always been recognized and accepted as the experts.

Service companies, in grappling with the same basic need for quality improvement, are experiencing similar problems of functional indifference and professional independence that have challenged manufacturing companies. And just like in manufacturing, these obstacles mostly occur in professional staff support areas as opposed to production operations. This confirms the belief of most quality professionals that poor quality and generally poor overall performance is at least 80 percent the result of the process and its planning and support, not of the operators.

The challenges of these new demands for staff quality improvement have not come alone. There are many helpful approaches for their accomplishment. In the battle for the minds of these professional staff people, their generally defensive attitudes might otherwise be too difficult to overcome. Actually, the American quality revolution for manufacturing and service companies comprises a proliferation of ideas and techniques aimed at these administrative and support functions. And it has been carefully promoted as an exciting new business venture and not a rehash of the perennial push for rejuvenated quality control. For an overview of this difference, see Figure 1–1.

From the many and varied company experiences that have been publicly shared in this decade-long pursuit of quality improvement, some central ideas have emerged.

FIGURE 1–1
What Is Companywide Quality Improvement?

It Is the Challenge of:	It Is Not:
A permanent quality solution; a new way of industrial life	Another quick-fix or rehash of the old qualitiy clichés
A new management philosophy	Another new quality program
Breakthrough thinking	Refixing the same old problems
A disciplined approach to problem solving	Fire fighting and other face-saving exercises
Nourishment by management actions and *team* results	Nourishment by posters, slogans, and false promises
A long-term unrelenting crusade	A short-term, expedient solution

Entrepreneurship

The main thrust of efforts to promote staff quality improvement has been for each staff or support function to look upon itself as a separate, independent business, selling its service to the company for a profit. Thus envisioned, the company is able to face the reality that if its internal staff groups had to be competitive in the external marketplace, some of them would not survive—most specifically because of inadequate or poor quality performance.

The rationale for this attempted breakthrough is that the needs and expectations of staff function customers, whether they be internal or external to the company, are not being satisfactorily fulfilled. Staffs are failing to establish appropriate provisions for their customers' actual needs: they are failing to conform to their own stated intent: and they are failing to anticipate changing conditions that call for adjustments to their game plan. And they are doing this in the light of rising customer expectations, increased personalization of the marketplace and the workplace, and rising antibusiness feelings of employees and end customers alike.

The recipient of each staff function's output—more often than not, an internal customer—can judge a function's performance through two benchmark measures:

1. The technical adequacy of the service being provided; in other words, how well does it satisfy the technical needs of the customer?
2. The timeliness and completeness of the service being provided; or how well does it satisfy the actual day-to-day productive needs of the customer?

Unhappy internal customers come into being each time an employee experiences an undesirable or upsetting happening, for example, receiving a late, incomplete, or unreasonably discrepant service as an integral part of their own work process. Such an occurrence does not normally represent a total failure on the part of the responsible party; rather, it is an unsatisfactory work situation as measured by the recipient's own personal quality performance standards and expectations. As a result of many such experiences, the internal worker/customer, who does not have the option to go elsewhere, loses motivation or, at the very least, becomes disenchanted with the real motives of the company. The entrepreneurial function thereby has a built-in major improvement opportunity.

The underlying cause for the continued occurrences of internal customer dissatisfaction is that individuals in staff support areas—managers, supervisors, and workers—are much too free to set their own standards of performance. Under these circumstances, the individual standards practiced are not likely to be either consistent or to be based on clearly defined internal customer needs and expectations. Such individuals are not unlike the doctors and lawyers who sometimes believe it is enough just to know their medicine or law.

Any given individual performance could just as well be motivated by a professionally superior or defensive attitude, a narrow-minded functional bias, the circumstances of one's personal life, or current personal feelings about the company. This, of course, is *not* the way management wants things to happen. And yet, without getting into why, adverse situations do occur in administrative and support staff work activities that clearly hinder profitability and competitiveness.

For staff and support functions to become truly competitive in an entrepreneurial sense, what's generally needed, for starters, is a gross strategic redirection of the company. This includes an instantaneous attitude change that:

- Demands all requirements be taken seriously.
- Accepts that mistakes are avoidable, recurring mistakes are unacceptable, and root causes of mistakes must be eliminated.

Rather than merely waiting or hoping for improvements, a company needs to be *transformed*, starting with each identified function being totally committed to the following three mandates:

1. Accomplishment of a complete agreement with each internal or external customer organization on exactly what is to be supplied. For example, the operations department needs from the product or service design department not only a design that will function as a customer offering, but a design that can be produced within the current capabilities of the production processes and within the cost limitations imposed by the marketing plan.

2. A valid, organized set of processes through which the agreed-upon requirements can be achieved. For example, it is not enough for the sales department to give their expert guess as to what the sales figures will be. There must be an organized market research process to give validity to these numbers, upon which so much important planning is based.

3. Established staff disciplines that are effectively utilized to assure that the needed processes are carried out as planned.

This approach to quality improvement—and that's exactly what it is—is easier said than done. But look at what is likely to happen if it is pursued. All administrative and support functions will have to communicate directly with their internal customers to determine and clearly establish *actual* customer requirements. This alone will help to eliminate those sticky problems where the internal customer's expectations and the provider's ability to provide are unwittingly far apart. This approach will also cause each support function to decide what its business really is and isn't, thereby eliminating, once and for all, those interfunctional miscalculations, misrepresentations, and just plain disagreements that otherwise contribute to waste and growing disillusionment.

Agreements reached between a support staff and its customers should be documented—that is, there should be no doubt about what is to be delivered and what constitutes its availability, timeliness, and completeness. This means that staff support organizations must communicate continuously with their internal customers.

Actual accomplishment of this kind of healthy relationship will spontaneously create interfunctional teamwork, and it will reinforce the need for each support staff to have organized processes through which it prepares and delivers its output. Later in this growth process, the disciplines required to ensure consistent service will evolve as a result of actively seeking quality improvement within the process. This entire concept of entrepreneurship—with its involvement of internal customer agreements, organized support processes, and disciplines—has been and remains a prime starting point for the development and promotion of companywide quality improvement.[6]

For it is your business, when the wall next door catches fire.

Horace

The Work Process

The next theme in the evolution of companywide quality improvement in the white-collar environment, says William J. McCabe, is to identify and focus on the work process.[7] This is the key available source of sustainable quality progress. All work done in an administrative or staff support organization can be viewed as being part of a work process, and processes can be understood, measured, and controlled.

Staff processes can be considered as follows:

1. Unique processes performed by individuals within an organization—such as the storeroom clerk, the laboratory technician, the crane operator, or the company nurse.
2. Functional processes whose major elements all report to a single manager—such as the marketing manager, the service or product design manager, the product planning manager, the production operations manager, the service operations manager(s), or the purchasing manager.
3. Business processes whose major elements are spread across several managers—such as production logistics and scheduling, management information systems, project management, personnel administration, or finance management.

The bulk of support processes will fall in the general category of functional processes, where a single manager is responsible. Each one of these major functions, however, can be composed of any number of individual work processes—such as the purchase order process within the overall purchasing process, the drawing preparation standard process within the product design function, the order-taking process within the marketing/sales function, and processes assigned to individuals (such as, for example, the auditor or the safety engineer).

For each category of functional processes, ownership and accountability for process results is almost always clearly established with the functional manager. This makes it easy to pursue quality improvement in clear functional responsibility paths. Business-process quality improvement can be pursued in exactly the same way, if ownership, represented by accountability for results, is established with the manager responsible for the required coordination.

The idea behind the focus on processes is that the ultimate success of companywide quality improvement depends on the collective improvement of all work processes. This, in turn, depends on the ability of each functional manager to identify the internal customers for each functional process, to agree on each customer's valid requirements, and to be organized to meet these requirements, all through a clear definition and control of the work processes involved. Ditto for the business managers.

If any function cannot satisfactorily accomplish the agreed-upon requirements, the functional manager must immediately initiate specific upgrade efforts to improve the process. In those cases where applicable methodology is not available, new methods must be developed. This initial effort at obviously needed improvement will become an important avenue for the creation of necessary and unique company techniques or applications, normally requiring the inputs and support of the company's quality professionals.

Sometimes just making the right effort is enough. Some years ago a major space program experienced a problem with its erector locking in a fail-safe mode part way up after a dry run. The astronauts had to be removed with the help of a cherry picker. Unable to be reproduced, the failure was ultimately written off as an anomaly. Then one day, before the entire world on national TV, a scheduled launch had to be scrubbed when the erector locked up on its way down.

As a direct result of this embarrassing incident, the division quality professional, with the help of support engineering, was given the responsibility and the authority to do "whatever it takes for this to *never* happen again." Now, the effort was *serious*, and several good things happened:

- A thorough design review of the erector system resulted in several design changes that eliminated unnecessary complexities. It also determined that the key system components could be thoroughly tested as part of the countdown operation without requiring actual movement of the erector, which no one previously thought was feasible.

- An in-depth analysis of functional failure modes, coupled with practical plans for recovery from each potential failure, led to a new countdown position that would have the system functioning again in less than ten minutes in the unfortunate event of a future failure.

- The incident never happened again, either in a dry run or on national TV.

Process Evaluation

At the beginning of any movement toward quality improvement for staff support areas, it will soon become clear that evaluations of staff performance against a clear set of requirements is a new phenomenon for most staff managers and their people. And it will be at least somewhat unwelcome because it tends to generate disagreements with their professional judgments and hampers their freedom to act on those judgments. Even the very fact of clearly established requirements will be new to many. But that is exactly why this action is so beneficial. Most professional areas have not been looked at in this way for a long time, if ever, and almost all of them will be ripe for short-range, obvious improvements.

As a bonus for the simple act of challenging each staff support work process to meet necessary quality performance requirements, obvious improvement opportunities will immediately begin to materialize, especially if the challenge is accompanied by questions like the following:

1. Is the process normally understood and executed exactly as planned and expected by staff management?

2. Is there consistency or considerable variation in the way it is being executed?

3. Are there steps in the process that are no longer needed?
4. Are all involved paperwork functions (i.e., preparing, reading, recording, interpreting, filing, and maintaining) currently necessary?

In all work situations where individual processes are not periodically shaken down for value, problems of the types indicated by these additional questions will almost always occur over time. In fact, the cost of such built-in inefficiencies—irregular performance, excessive variation, unnecessary operations, and nonessential paperwork—becomes buried in the normal cost of doing business; it remains hidden until decreasing profitability or stiff competition forces a reevaluation of the status quo or until a wise management decides for quality improvement.

Throughout the entire history of manufacturing quality programs and the growing base of knowledge about service quality improvement, there has been a discernable pattern of events surrounding the quality upgrade of existing jobs and processes. There has almost always been abundant opportunities to eliminate unnecessary subtasks and to suggest the application of readily available simplification techniques. Such opportunities exist because individual job and work-process standards have traditionally been weak or lacking. And *any lack of exacting job standards always allows the spawning of excess variations and widespread inefficiencies in performance.*

Process Management and Improvement

After a company has acted to evaluate and challenge the integrity of its work processes, the next step is process management and improvement. This is the main event, where the structural work of quality improvement begins. All events leading to this crucial point in management decision making have been the preliminaries.

To theorize the idea of process management, consider any work process to be an operation or combination of operations, with each operation defined as a set of interrelated work tasks, and each task having prescribed inputs and outputs. For example, a short-order cook's basic task is to prepare a meal, the output, from inputs of customer order, recipe, and ingredients. We all know the kind of problems that can occur with this relatively simple business endeavor. Consider then the enormous possibilities for error in the more complex processes of industry.

Quality management of work processes, or defined sets of operations, means identification and measurement of select, strategic results. It involves measuring performance, identifying performance problems, determining root causes of problems, and taking appropriate corrective action to achieve break-through improvement where possible—that is, to achieve continuous process

FIGURE 1-2
Work-Process Quality Improvement

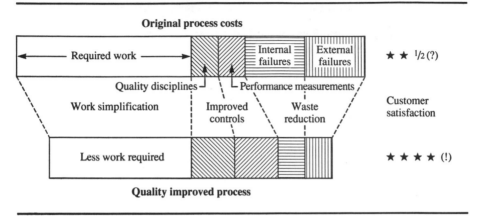

Source: William J. McCabe, "Examining Processes Improves Operations," *Quality Progress,* July
1989, pp. 26–32. Adapted by permission.

improvement incrementally. *This is the basic improvement strategy that is at the heart of all improvement programs.*

Figure 1-2 clearly shows the potential for improvement that exists in any process that is not receiving the current benefits of formal quality improvement. It shows a reduction and simplification of required work, improved process measurement and control, and a significant amount of waste reduction; all of which leads to a substantial improvement in customer satisfaction.

The first problem normally encountered in the application of quality improvement techniques to administrative and support functions, says Eugene H. Melan, is that the processes are often ill-defined, poorly documented, and unmeasured.[8] As a result, there is a lack of knowledge about how these processes really work, how effective they are, and whether or not performance is getting better or worse.

If this condition exists to any significant degree, it should be obvious that before companies can pursue performance measurements and corrective action, they must first clearly define the administrative and support processes in question, assign ownership responsibilities, and unquestionably establish the boundaries of responsibility with other functions. For administrative and support groups unaccustomed to well-defined work tasks or formal process steps, these will be difficult efforts. For many companies, merely addressing and challenging this untidy condition will become a test of the true mettle of management's quality commitment.

Once the administrative and support processes have been defined, the next business task is to determine the most meaningful measures of process results and effectiveness. That is, to focus on questions like:

1. How adequately is this process meeting its requirements?
2. What is the true capability of this process?
3. Where should improvement efforts be focused?

In seeking to answer these questions, you will discover that before attempting to control or improve a process, you must first understand it. Further, you will see that before trying to control every parameter of every process, you must find out what's most important about each process.

The best way to understand a process is to learn about variability. All processes produce variable outcomes, and this variability will occur in two categories. The first category is *special causes*—sources of variability that aren't always present, like a worn-out tool or inadequate training. The root causes of this type of variability can be discovered and eliminated without having to change the process.

The second category of variability in a process is *common causes*, the sources of which are inherent to the process itself. These variations—like normal tool wear, material input fluctuations, or personal skill differences—comprise the factors that limit the inherent capability of a process. When these factors are operating within their optimum and the special causes have been eliminated or minimized, the process is "in control." This means that the only way it can be further improved is by investing in better equipment, materials, software, maintenance, and so forth—that is, by *changing the process*.

Ideally, a process will be "in control" and capable of meeting all its requirements. It is much more likely, however, that one or both of the following conditions will exist, presenting the opportunity for immediate remedial action:

1. The process is not capable of meeting the agreed-upon requirements of its customer; it therefore must be changed.
2. The process is capable of meeting its requirements but it is "out of control"—that is, it is inconsistently or incompletely achieving the required results.

Once the work processes are understood, and there is knowledge of the need for and a commitment to process improvement, it will become clear that many different approaches to accomplishing that improvement are available. Some techniques and methodologies have been specifically developed for staff support functions. Each unique process situation will dictate for itself which improvement method or methods are likely to be the most effective. The bottom line is to clearly define and understand the administrative and support processes, then to evaluate the tools available before finalizing a specific action plan for process control and improvement.[9]

Based on actual experience, a common denominator, or universal framework, for the detailed development of companywide plans should include the following features:

- Make quality improvement ongoing and relentless.
- Customize it to your organization.
- Involve all personnel.
- Keep people informed and educated.
- Recognize and applaud progress.

SUMMARY

The quality challenge of the marketplace during the 1980s took direct aim at the companywide operations of American businesses, a challenge unceasingly intensified with advancing worldwide quality progress. This challenge, in addition to being the catalyst for important product quality improvements, focused on quality improvement in the staff support and service functions of manufacturing companies and all functions of the service business. Its initiative has been to compel all functional organizations to stand alone, reexamine, and totally justify their contributions to integrated company performance and profitability.

This functional self-appraisal, in turn, led to a detailed scrutiny of the work process, or the way in which these functions are being accomplished. Companies then had to come to grips with the realities that significantly affect the limits and control of process performance. But while much progress has been achieved, many of the opportunities identified turned out *easier to acknowledge than to resolve*.

To a very large degree, the idea of companywide quality improvement was successful in leading many companies to envision the potential for genuine improvement. However, too many attempts to proceed got bogged down in the unfolding realization that functional and interfunctional responsibilities for quality—basic company quality responsibilities—were either missing altogether, completely misunderstood, totally unacceptable, or deliberately ignored. Without these responsibilities being clearly established and accepted, it was too easy to shirk the demanding obligations of quality improvement and to point the finger elsewhere.

CHAPTER 2

THE RESPONSIBILITIES FOR QUALITY

Understanding and accepting the value of entrepreneurial thinking, the need for detailed staff process definitions and controls, and the involvement of staff personnel in functional quality improvement, as previously discussed, is one thing. Getting it incorporated into the woodwork of staff functions is something else.

When open to the improvement opportunities potentially available, functional managers may also recognize that fundamental functional responsibilities for quality—the basis upon which interfunctional quality improvement development decisions will acutely rest—are not clearly understood nor established as an integral part of their assigned missions. This confusion about the basic responsibilities for quality has been confirmed over and over again through surveys of top management conducted for the American Society for Quality Control (ASQC).

Bridging these gaps in the *meaning of quality* has proven to be a difficult but important undertaking in itself. In effect, this specific complication has occasioned the evolution of companywide quality improvement to occur in stages. The understanding and acceptance of fundamental business responsibilities for quality is a prerequisite stage.

THE MEANING OF QUALITY

No matter which road a company travels in the pursuit of quality improvement, it must address three crucial elements:

1. The definition of quality for the company.
2. The establishment of product or service quality standards unique to the company and its business.

3. The clear incorporation of responsibilities for quality performance throughout the entire company.

The meaning of quality, as represented by these three basic yardsticks, has been the Achilles' heel of quality progress from the inception of quality control programs—when the best that could be hoped for was a decent inspection prior to delivery—right up to the present. Contrary to popular opinion, quality does not automatically occur when work is finished, as in "ready for delivery"; nor when it is merely an opinion that the finished work is OK—as in "functional," "usable," or in the worst case scenario, "good enough."

Quality is not what the planning and producing individuals may think or wish it to be. It is exactly what exists in the mind of the customer when he or she receives and personally appraises the product or service. This includes the internal customer, recipient of internal support service or work in process, as well as the external customer. In short, the meaning of quality is directly related to *customer satisfaction;* it is still best defined as "conformance to customer requirements." Any other definition for quality leaves too much room for interpretation and bias, making it impossible to work with—and yet there were companies, during the eighties, who obviously made the mistake of thinking they could pursue quality improvement with a less severe or less demanding definition.

Even this customer-oriented approach is not faultless. Some customers will have unrealistic expectations about what they should be receiving—thinking "champagne and caviar" in a "beer and hotdog" environment—in either the marketplace or the workplace. While this condition cannot be completely avoided, except internally, it is reasonable to expect that this gross miscalculation is not generally the case.

The people who form the total customer base today are more sophisticated, better educated, more discriminating, more streetwise, and more demanding than ever before, and they are not difficult to understand. Companies must be fully aware of these facts since the customers, when solicited, are the most important input to company quality standards.

Understanding the internal customer poses a different challenge from that of the external customer, and it is much easier to achieve. Employees want to be listened to, and they are an untapped reservoir of the most intimate knowledge about how work is really accomplished—about what standards do exist, where there is an existing need for standards, and when standards are not consistently maintained.

The "customer first" conceptual approach to the definition of quality suggests that a company bases all its quality standards, or performance standards, on the customers' requirements. This starts with the end customer and works back up the direct and support work-process paths through all internal customers. It also suggests that these standards be established in each and every company operation as an essential ingredient for *consistency* in the satisfaction of all customers. Lest you be misled by not viewing this task in its proper perspective, setting quality standards means being committed to paying careful attention to details because that is what the customer notices; and it is always wrong to assume or guess what the customer really needs or expects.

Quality Standards

To understand the meaning of a quality standard, consider these two aspects of its definition:

1. Quality standards and company standards of operation are one and the same thing. Quality standards are not additional requirements to be met or not met as conditions warrant. They are the absolute requirements for performance or results that the company expects of its employees, and they are usually found in documents like job descriptions, work-process definitions, function responsibilities, and product- or service-offering specifications. When any of these documents is weak on quality, or quality standards are missing altogether, the opportunities for inadequate quality performance are great.

2. Determining exact customer requirements for use in establishing quality standards is not a black-and-white process. In the eyes of the customer, internal and external, perception is everything. How a product or support service is perceived by its recipient may be different from how it is perceived by its supplier. Recognizing, studying, and bridging these gaps of perception, when they exist, is a delicate and important judgmental part of the standard-setting process.

In reviewing the quality trends of the eighties, it's difficult to understand why the setting of quality standards continues to be the underlying problem it has been over the years; it's usually the first thing that quality professionals and consultants speak about. Is it somehow still plausible that managers would rather assume people ''know'' what to do than to spell it out for them in fine detail?

What ever happened to the experienced manager who could work any job within the organization being managed? While there are not too many of these managers around anymore, we can be thankful that more and more companies are learning the business value of quality standards. Also on the plus side, today's pioneering companies are sharing the good news about quality standards and quality improvement with the entire industrial world. An old adage says it all:

Real quality is the presence of value—and not just the absence of defects.

FUNCTIONAL RESPONSIBILITIES FOR QUALITY

To understand what is meant by the basic functional responsibilities for quality, and their intrinsic business value, consider the following questions about each function:

- How does this function's work output affect the overall quality perception of the company's internal work performance and its outgoing products or service?

- Who determines *what* internal quality standards are needed by this function?

- How many preventable interfunctional deficiencies are being routinely tolerated, simply because there is no convenient way to expose and eliminate them?

Unless a company is considerably advanced in its pursuit of quality improvement, the answers to these questions will normally confirm a serious lack of understanding among key functions regarding the meaning and relative importance of quality as it specifically affects their work processes and responsibilities. In this regard, a company is its own worst enemy when it allows each function to march to its own drummer. From a basic business point of view, there is a fundamental need to have clearly defined quality responsibilities built into each function's charter. The overall intent is to have each function lined up, in exactly the same direction, in total support of *company quality objectives.*

To get some feel for the extent of this problem, let's explore what's happening in key staff support areas. But first, let's appreciate some major differences between staff support or service functions and the production operations function:

1. Support services cannot be centrally produced and stockpiled for future use. They are almost always produced for one time, immediate consumption, having instant impact on the user's process.

2. The user of the support service normally has a critical role to play in the fulfillment of the service. His or her expectations about the service are crucial in achieving satisfactory utilization.

In the light of these differences, *any* support service that is not exactly right will create a situation, either hidden or obvious, that is detrimental and costly to a company. Failure to complete any one of the more important staff support functions (like the marketing plan or product/service definition) "right the first time" will always have a more serious impact on the business than almost any amount of operations problems, almost all of which are considerably easier to resolve. Once cast in concrete, for example, a marketing specification or product/service design deficiency may have to exist for the life of the project because it was the basis for major project investments.

A keen awareness of these important differences, and the knowledge that everyday staff performance can be the root cause of serious but preventable business problems, should sufficiently motivate companies to endorse this prerequisite stage of CWQI program development.

The Marketing Function

Since the marketing function, including sales, is fundamentally responsible for determining exactly what new or modified product/service offerings the marketplace is calling for, it represents the very first step in the establishment of quality requirements for a company's new or expanded business opportunities. Marketing's definition of this new business, commonly termed a *marketing specification,* is the starting point for ensuing design and production efforts. Wholly and clearly establishing this initial and most strategic stake in the ground for the future business of the company is marketing's most important quality responsibility.

Even before the advent of quality improvement, marketing has been, or should have been, accountable for how well it describes the real needs of the customer. In addition, the marketing function should provide clear readings on how well satisfied current customers are with:

1. The quality of the company's products or service.
2. The administration of the company's advertising, contracts, user documents, customer relations, and distribution systems, and the handling of customer complaints and problems.

Facing up to these more obvious marketing-unique quality responsibilities is a major goal in the thrust for quality improvement in the marketing and sales functional area.

In the world of quality progress, truly changing the quality role and responsibilities of any professional function, like marketing, from where it has become entrenched in the typical American business culture is no easy task (see Figure 2–1). The status quo is a formidable foe in short-range–thinking business environments. But thanks to the saving grace and motivating power of worldwide quality competition, it is being tackled and successfully overcome—albeit, ever so slowly. The need to turn up the volume of progress is one of the principal reasons this book was written.

Any successful approach to the conversion of marketing to the world of quality improvement starts by recognizing the function as a crucial part of a companywide system to achieve customer satisfaction. Marketing normally has more direct contact with outside customers, through sales, market research, and customer service, than any other function. On the other hand, few marketing personnel are thought to have a respectable understanding of their formidable

FIGURE 2–1

Dunagin's people

"OUR QUALITY CONTROL IS OUT OF CONTROL AND PRODUCT FAILURE IS AT AN ALL-TIME HIGH. CLEARLY, THE THING TO DO IS INCREASE OUR ADVERTISING BUDGET."

Source: *The Orlando Sentinel*, April 18, 1986, p. A-19. Reprinted by permission.

quality responsibilities; for the most part, they view quality problems as an operations responsibility. From this practical starting point, marketing can be helped into the following areas of functional responsibility.

Marketing Specification

As previously mentioned, the foremost quality responsibility of the marketing function is the marketing specification, or project definition, as it is sometimes called. The two worst case scenarios for the output of this responsibility are:

1. Specifications arrived at more through opinions than hard facts.
2. Specifications that are so loosely established it will be easy for areas other than marketing to be held accountable for any future lack of success.

To avoid any inclination toward either of these two directions, the marketing specification must clearly:

- Be a functional specification—that is, within clear cost limitations, a definition of exactly what the product or service is supposed to look like and do, including necessary supplemental requirements (such as product reliability or durability: or specific patterns of behavior for service deliveries).
- Be firmly supported by pertinent facts from past company field experience, customer communications, current market surveys, and recent competitor evaluations.
- Require the inputs and concurrence of other critically involved functions—such as product/service development, production operations, purchasing, quality, planning, and finance—in the final document.

In "the good old days," it was sufficient to deliver "what we thought the customer wanted" or "what we thought the customer was willing to pay for." But with the advent of modern-day quality competition, this easy and rather callous approach had to change. Now you must determine what the customer has the right to expect. If you don't, your company will find itself on the outside looking in, while the competition is meeting these expectations.

Sometimes, when a company has been the sales leader for a particular product or service for many years, ongoing market study does not seem as important as it did in the beginning. One small company, for example, led in the housing market sales of heating system parts for several decades. This company truly enjoyed having the standard for the industry. But their standard was a Cadillac in a market that was becoming more and more price conscious.

One day, quite unexpectedly, a new, smaller but equivalent product appeared in the marketplace, sold by a foreign competitor for nearly half the going price. The net result was that the standard bearer company was caught short and forced into an immediate, expedited new design effort. In time, they managed to regain much of their former market share—but, oh what it cost them in added expense and reputation! The moral of this story is that it always costs more to play catch-up than it does to lead; however, being a leader means always paying close attention to what the marketplace is saying.

Once established, the marketing specification will be the keystone quality reference for all involved functions. All other product or service quality responsibilities will flow from or be a derivative of this one.

Customer Communication System

At the other end of the marketing function, there is a clear responsibility to know the true status of customer satisfaction and to assure that it receives continued prime attention. Marketing can fulfill this quality responsibility by establishing and effectively utilizing a formal *customer communication system* for problem reporting, returned goods, complaints, compliments, inquiries, and other communications.

To be effective, the customer communication system must provide timely responses; also, it must include appropriate documentation, analysis, corrective action, and follow-up communication to ensure acceptable resolution. For the company to remain competitive, marketing cannot allow any customer communications to be ignored—or any responses to be deficient—through any lack of identification, organization, or discipline in their execution. In essence, marketing must become the quality leader for all contacts with the customer.

Guidelines for customer communications should always include the following:

1. Make certain you instruct your customers to sufficiently understand your products or services, how to properly experience them, and how to contact you if dissatisfied.

2. Make certain you acknowledge complaints and resolve them promptly, courteously, fairly, and ungrudgingly. One true test of service quality excellence today is, "What happens under adverse circumstances?"

3. Make certain you prevent the *recurrence* of customer problems through internal feedback, education, and corrective action.

4. Make certain your products or services are safe and in compliance with all applicable laws, regulations, and industrial or commercial standards.

5. Make certain that everything you say or publish about your products or services is accurate, in good taste, and understandable.

6. Make certain that you routinely solicit and *listen* to what your customers have to say.

During the development phase of new projects, interfunctional reviews are often conducted as an integral part of another function's mission and responsibility—functions such as development, purchasing, or operations planning. At all such meetings, marketing should be accountable to *represent the customer*.

Using the marketing specification as its bible, marketing is responsible for evaluating other functions' planning progress in terms of its ultimate impact on customer satisfaction. Marketing must challenge all potential failures to meet the established specification requirements; it must also be prepared to negotiate necessary changes, sometimes caused by unmet functional expectations on the one hand and unexpected improvement opportunities on the other. Ideally, every function is expected to think "customer first"; but of course, their basic attitude will almost always be biased as compared to marketing, which must remain 100 percent pure in its fidelity to the customer. The company's future is *not* to be put at risk.

Introduction of New Products or Services
Another area in which marketing has the prime company quality responsibility is the company's plan for formal *launching of a new product or service* into the marketplace. How this launch is planned and carried out will have great impact on the customers' initial acceptance of the new offering.

Normally, launching involves a coordinated process to ensure that the entire marketing organization, down to the last tier selling level, is properly prepared for the introduction. It must be armed with all the knowledge and support tools necessary to promote and to professionally support initial customer satisfaction. The quality of this preparation will often depend on how well marketing coordinates the inputs and involvement of other participating functions.

Quality Review of Contract
Winning the big contract is always an important part of sales strategy, but sometimes the excitement of the win serves to camouflage the small print in the contract, particularly as it might apply to the inclusion of customer-specific operations or support-process quality requirements. Unfortunately, the inadvertent neglect of these inclusions sometimes leads to unachievable or costly commitments. Marketing can prevent this type of situation from ever developing by utilizing an interfunctional *quality review of contract* prior to formal agreement. This problem-prevention activity entails calling on all available company expertise.

Quality Review of Advertising
When preparing advertising literature, it is always good to put your best foot forward; but there also seems to be a strong tendency to exaggerate a bit. Normally there is no harm, but if products or services become involved in a

serious problem, everything about them becomes important. This is especially critical in America today where advertising, public relations, and image-making have become a fine art. Some people don't seem to think they have to "do the right thing" anymore to be profitable—rather, they merely have to make customers "think" they are.

The truth is that all misrepresentations will work against a company in the hands of its accusers. The best way for marketing to prevent the problem of unintended express warranties and other problems with advertisements, catalogs, and sales brochures is to require, just as with contracts, an interfunctional *quality review of advertising* prior to release, making certain that a representative from the legal department participates.

There are other areas of quality responsibility for the marketing function, but it is not the intent here to cover all possibilities. For product companies, replacement parts availability for delivery close to the user's needs, for example, could be an important quality element—considering that the lack of timeliness and quality of spare parts could result in a loss of repeat sales. If a distribution system is part of the operation, it goes without saying that any modification or repair service will require the strictest incorporation of quality assurance measures. The same is true for service agreements and express warranties.

Setting the Stage for Quality

The pattern to be established here—and followed by other functions—is that by first establishing specific marketing function responsibilities for quality that may have been deficient or loosely considered in the past, the stage is set to truly build quality into the marketing function. Marketing and sales personnel can then become fully aware of the crucial value of quality to the business. This, in turn, lays the necessary groundwork for the introduction of formal quality improvement into all areas of marketing and sales work.

Achieving a clear quality direction for each function within a company also sets the stage for individual functions to recognize and understand the potential impact other functions can have on their own ability to achieve quality results. For example, marketing will see that its market share dreams can easily go up in smoke if product or service development and production operations are not truly committed to their functional quality responsibilities; that is, if they do not achieve the quality performance that marketing expects. Development and production operations, on the other hand, will come to realize that the very best efforts on their part will *not* overcome a poorly conceived marketing specification. Realizations like this should be enough to entice all key functions to want to become firmly entrenched on the company quality team.

Later in the quality improvement process, marketing will be able to see the potential impact of other functions' quality successes on the achievement level of the marketing plan; for example, the potential of an exceptional quality design and consistent production quality performance to contribute to unexpected sales growth and future marketing expectations. In making this connection, marketing will also discover the unique opportunity it has to influence the performance of others within the framework of a company quality program—and people in the marketing function will develop a taste for the experience. They may even discover just how easy it is to tear down burdensome interfunctional fences when quality is the activator. This it the exact path through which some functional leaders become highly influential company quality leaders.

> *Grace is given of God, but* knowledge *is bought in the market.*
>
> Arthur Hugh Clough

New or Improved Product/Service Development

Without a steady flow of new customer offerings, companies are hard-pressed to sustain a steady growth pattern. The richness of the growth, however, depends to a large degree on the quality of design for the new business, even when the new business is merely a different application or variation of old business. That is, it depends on the degree to which a new product or service, produced in conformance to its design or formal definition, truly satisfied the customers' expectations—assuming for the moment, of course, that marketing was "right on" when preparing the new marketing specification.

If the ensuing development entity is marginal or deficient, it will have a devastating effect on project profit plans. On the other hand, a well-designed new offering will enhance its own reputation and profit potential. *Real quality has a way of creating its own image.* What better reason to build distinct quality responsibilities into the new business development function.

To understand the challenge of integrating clear-cut quality responsibilities into the processes of new product or service development, let's examine who does this work and what it is they do. Depending on the scope of technology involved, the organizations responsible for development generally cover a wide variety of activities ranging from studies of fundamental scientific and commercial breakthroughs pertinent to the company's business, to the actual design of new product or service offerings. This puts them in an elite class within the company—owner and protector of that essence of knowledge most crucial for sustaining the flow of innovations that keeps the company in business.

The people who do this development work, says George J. Kidd, Jr., are generally well educated, creative, and adequately compensated.[1] They believe that the company's technological successes are mostly due to their own efforts, even though their performance is almost never measured to any real degree. Consequently, their prestige and motivations are often more related to professional peer recognition and approval than to acknowledgments from within the company. Accustomed to exercising considerable self-direction, they would find the thought of relinquishing any of their freedom to be totally abhorrent. Overcoming these formidable obstacles is a slow and tedious process; but the major benefit, over the long haul, is that you may get to stay in business.

The principal output of most development organizations is information, usually in the form of product or service technical descriptions, specifications, and support documents. While the quality of the documentation is important, the information contained in the documents is of primary concern to the quality of design.

To assess the quality of technical information, a classic quality question must be asked: "Is it fit for its intended use?" Does it give its customers—in this case, the internal company users of this information—what they need to fulfill their responsibilities? To satisfactorily answer this question on a continuous basis, the development organization must accept responsibility for the satisfaction of internal company customers rather than be content with their own personal satisfactions. In other words, the development leaders must, in fact, become an integral part of the company quality team. They cannot be left as an island unto themselves.

Fundamentally, establishing quality responsibilities within the development function is entirely aimed at perfecting the development effort and preventing outright development deficiencies or errors, all of which are costly to customer acceptance and future sales. More specifically, designers must take responsibility for the inherent quality of their work output, utilizing, as appropriate, the tools of quality control and improvement that have been created specifically for their function.[2] In a practical business sense, the chief designer should never be surprised to learn that the output of the development group turned out to be either exceptionally good or terribly inadequate.

Development Qualification

A good starting point for discussing development function quality responsibilities is *development qualification.* This is an activity specifically designed to verify overall development accomplishment. Just like a final product test or service audit is utilized to verify that all production operations have been successfully accomplished prior to delivery and acceptance by customers, a qualification exercise is intended to verify that all development actions have been successfully accomplished prior to the release of the new product or service definition for full production planning and operations. The business value of development qualification is simply that the problems it discovers and resolves would be much more costly if not discovered until the production operations phase, or worse, until acceptance and use by the customer.

More specifically, qualification of a new development is the formal testing or auditing of prototype or pilot-run offerings, utilizing production equipment and processes to the greatest extent possible. The purpose of this exercise is to ensure that the new offering, as defined, conforms to every one of its detail requirements—usually comprising the marketing specification, applicable definition documents, and any standard production processes that are an integral part of the definition.

Once a new product or service offering has been qualified, the company should review the need to requalify, by repeating some or all of the qualification exercise, on an annual or biannual basis and after any major design change. The reason for periodic requalification is that company products and services usually do not remain identical to those that were initially qualified. Inconspicuous changes can enter into supplies, processes, and the way in which products or services are finished for delivery. These subtle changes, in time, may cause a discernable change in customer satisfaction. The extent to which this can happen may vary widely for different lines of business, but it is always less costly to prevent.

Development Reviews

While the basic purpose of development qualification is to provide assurance that all is right with the new development, actual practice at times will reveal a major weakness. Instead of the design refinements that might normally be expected, some programs are actually thrown into a tailspin as a result of major qualification failures. A proven way to avoid such costly failures and, at the same time, to maximize assurance of development success is the effective use of formal *development reviews*—the most important development quality responsibility for perfecting the new offering.

A development review program requires periodic reviews of development progress. The marketing, production planning, purchasing, production operations, and other involved functions periodically assess whether satisfactory progress is being made *before* continuing with the development effort. The purpose is to ensure that the end result meets or betters cost and performance requirements. For service companies, where the development effort may not be as complicated as designing a new product and may, in fact, be considered a strictly independent function, this discipline will probably appear as a new concept. It is, however, one of the most important quality concepts to be learned from the most advanced manufacturing companies.

Development reviews start with the original new offering idea—an introduction from the development leaders to other involved functions—and continue until a "complete definition" review releases the development for qualification samples (pilot products or prototype services). Within this framework, specific development review meetings are planned and scheduled. They focus on achievements and a consensus readiness to proceed. But they are also utilized to manage and control necessary trade-offs between key development parameters, such as product or service performance requirements, reliability, producibility, and unit cost.

If applicable development review efforts are planned, scheduled, budgeted, and executed for each new development, all involved functions can confidently enter into the development qualification exercise. Major failures or surprises will be limited to state-of-the-art conditions. Overall development costs will have been minimized, and the entire development effort will have been more effectively managed. There is no better way to enter a production commitment.

Other Quality Responsibilities
While development reviews and development qualification may offer a higher technical challenge, other quality responsibilities within the development function are equally important. Making sure that any test and measurement equipment being used is calibrated, for example, will eliminate errors between documented developmental results and their translation into actual new product or service performance requirements. Other development errors can be prevented by ensuring the quality of model shop work, and supplier parts, materials, and processing utilized in the development effort. An important internal control within the development function is the checking of technical documentation to ensure conformance to documentation standards and prevent obvious documentation errors.

A lack of discipline in any of these areas can lead to false impressions, unnecessary work, or costly investigations when measured results don't seem to correlate *after* the development has been released for qualification or production.

Development support to marketing is a significant effort for some companies (e.g., those with large design engineering organizations) and should always be an important quality responsibility for the development team. Without carefully conceived, technically accurate inputs to each new business plan, for example, marketing and company management could be committing to key business strategies on false hopes—simply because the development leaders had exaggerated their own abilities or the proven abilities of state-of-the-art technologies crucial to the company's business. For any development function, there can be no more grievous quality sin.

Development support to production is also a vital responsibility of the development function. It includes the management of development changes required to strengthen or improve production operations and the technical support of problem identification and resolution. From an overall company point of view, this is the time to wrap up any loose ends that may still be in the way of a smooth, profitable production operation. Capable technical support is crucial during this initial production period. Development organizations that have trouble providing this support, usually because their normal priorities are to quickly get on with the next new project, should be reminded that the production function is their *prime customer.*

Development support to production may sound easy, but in the manufacturing sector it can be the source for many costly quality deficiencies. For example, product design organizations, like most professional organizations, are almost never completely satisfied with the design at the required time for release to production. When these organizations lack clear-cut quality responsibilities and disciplines, they may continue a fatherly interest in design refinement during the early production phase—often at great cost to the company versus the actual added value of the refinement.

On the other hand, some design changes are expected and needed during early production efforts, such as fixing design deficiencies that are discovered and providing producibility support for the production process.

Again, depending on the specific quality responsibilities established and the realities of actual design deficiencies, true support for the manufacturing process can easily become obscured. For example, an extensive after-the-fact study conducted in one industrial products company reported the following ''reasons'' for design changes:

Reasons for Change	Support to Production	Design Rework
As stated	86%	14%
Reevaluation	31%	69%

The message here is obvious: When left to their own interpretation of responsibility, organizations will *favor* themselves at every opportunity—and management misses another opportunity to *know* the truth.

But the worst condition of all occurs when designers are free to guess at what's required to fix problems in production. An investigation at one consumer electronics plant into the cause of a seemingly persistent problem, affecting about 5 percent of a particular product line during final test, was instigated as part of a corporate review. It revealed a history of 27 engineering design changes specifically related to the problem. Two years and 27 design changes after discovery, the problem still existed. You can draw your own conclusion as to how this situation might relate to your own business.

Examples from the service industry include an insurance company being totally inflexible in response to their agents' spontaneous reaction to a newly designed policy, or a bank with the same negative attitude toward the special needs and wishes of individual customers. A restaurant might change its menu when it really needs to improve individual recipes, or a hotel might replace employees when the problem is employee training. The larger the organization, the more likely that new customer offerings will be well thought-out and systematically implemented; but they won't be as open and desirous of new knowledge from early production experiences, unless, of course, there was an immediate disaster.

What we have just discussed in this subsection are basic quality responsibilities for the new product or service development function. Many of these important responsibilities have become standard practice in the more advanced quality improvement-oriented companies. But in all too many industrial or commercial situations, there is a lack of understanding and commitment to these quality-of-design ideals for new customer offerings. Those organizations have a golden opportunity for improvement that should not be missed.

You can get rich by preventing defects.

Philip B. Crosby

Production Planning and Execution

The overall quality aim of production planning is to perfect the production process and prevent operating deficiencies or errors that would reduce customer satisfaction or increase costs. The extent to which this is accomplished can spell the difference between a mediocre and an outstanding production effort.

With so much knowledge and experience available today in the use of production process controls, it is inconceivable to think that production planning would start without a clear knowledge of current process capabilities and without including all necessary operator instructions and training. There is absolutely no excuse today for not having these specific quality responsibilities firmly established in the production planning function. And there is no reason to ever have to expect that any nonconforming product or service will be produced or prepared for delivery. Unfortunately, this is not generally the case.

An important but often overlooked responsibility for the production process is the *control of substitutions to and changes or deviations from the plan.* All too often the carefully thought-out plans for production operations are discarded when a serious obstacle occurs. Assumptions are made about substitutions or changes that would never be tolerated in the initial planning. What's needed is a quality discipline that requires all variations from the plan to be formally approved and verified for capability the same as the original process. The secret here is to anticipate such needs in the strategic plan for production and not let undue schedule pressures force mistakes that in the long run are more costly.

Another important and sometimes difficult discipline is the control of unauthorized work. All production personnel must be trained to work exactly in accordance with the production plan or cause the plan to be corrected to what is required. Deviating from work plan instructions can unwittingly cause or contribute to a new problem somewhere downstream in the operation. The resulting costs will almost always be excessive, since the cause of the problem—the unauthorized work—is unknown to the problem-solver and impossible to discover. Tolerating any unplanned or unauthorized work, therefore, is dangerous and must be formally condemned in production operations.

A classic lesson about unauthorized work was learned many years ago in an electronics assembly plant. An investigation into the cause of periodic final test failures led to the assembly process, where two assemblers were found to be force-fitting a particular subassembly with the help of an unauthorized rubber mallet, completely unaware of the effect this was having on some of the sensitive parts within the subassembly. It became evident, as the investigation continued, that the perception of work in the assembly area was oblivious to anything else except the immediate need for output. This type of situation in production operations is very likely to be encountered in the initial stages of any quality improvement venture.

Production planning must also recognize the importance of *calibration and maintenance* operations for all production equipment. A precisely planned and systematically executed calibration program provides confidence in the use of production data for acceptance or process adjustment decisions. Inadequate budget or attention to equipment maintenance can be the cause of serious quality deficiencies—from excess waste and rework caused by breakdowns that could have been prevented, to the development of marginal output conditions that may ultimately affect customer satisfaction.

For production operations to support quality progress, there must be a *commitment to quality* at least equal to the commitments to cost and schedule. Any gains in production objectives at the expense of quality are not gains for the company. They are paid for in reduced customer satisfaction and loss of future business. Quality must, therefore, be clearly established as a fundamental responsibility of the production operation.

The production manager or supervisor must realize that inadequate equipment, supplies, support services, training, work process instructions, and so forth are not allowed as excuses for inadequate quality results. Only when the production operation refuses to accept or condone deficient inputs or service can it exert improvement pressure on all support organizations. This is the way for production to act as its own catalyst in the perfecting of the production process.

An appropriate quality theme for production operations:

Things of quality have no fear of time.

The Purchasing Function

The complexity of today's business climate demands cooperation between purchasing and suppliers—a planned, continuing relationship based on mutual respect and the establishment of clear-cut quality responsibilities for both sides of the contract. Company accountability for supplier conformance to requirements must be clearly placed in the hands of the buyer; but the supplier, in turn, needs to be treated as a partner, with mutual trust as the basis for a continuous exchange of knowledge and ideas. Working together will eliminate the prevailing emphasis on supplier quick fixes for problems, and it can lead to genuine problem resolutions and future problem prevention.

On the buyer's side, an important supplier quality responsibility rests clearly in the hands of the people who define the *quality requirements for supplies*— normally the product/service development function or the technical arm of production planning. Experience in resolving supplier quality problems reveals that communication between buyer and supplier is often lacking in technical depth and clarity, an inevitable result of informal communication. The only way to avoid such disparities is to require each purchase order to contain complete, accurate, and clear technical information, and then to resolutely enforce a discipline of formal change control—that is, "No verbal changes!"

Prior to initial negotiation, suppliers must always be selected on the basis of their capability to meet price, delivery, and technical requirements. *Supplier evaluations* can be accomplished through formal survey data; or, as appropriate, the buyer can conduct an on-site evaluation to assess the supplier's production system—that is, to determine process capabilities, adequacy of controls, and level of training and qualification of the work force. Beyond that, if required, the buyer can evaluate the supplier's total management system. The days of "low bidder" as the only criterion are gone forever—along with the companies this policy has destroyed.

Supplier evaluation should be a two-way street. Some years ago a small switching company was one of three final bidders on the switchgear for a major government project. This was a big job for this company and if won, would have really put them on the map. In fact, they did not win the contract; but they did receive, as a formal part of the evaluations conducted, a thorough appraisal of their quality system. This was the one part of their highly ambitious new business efforts that seemed to be *left behind* when compared to all other key functions.

This company was so impressed with the deeper significance of the evaluation, they asked to bring their top management team to the prime contractor's facility for a more detailed feedback. This did happen, with the net result being that quality moved up to the head table at this forward-thinking, young company—never again to be taken lightly.

Suppliers must be told up front that quality is non-negotiable, and this principle must be followed up with *quality performance measurements and feedback*. These measurements should encompass the critical variables of quality, delivery, and total cost, which includes the cost impact of production difficulties traceable to the supplier's performance. The supplier must then be held accountable to investigate the root cause of reported problems and to take necessary corrective actions. An open and honest, two-way communication while accomplishing these disciplines will help to eliminate or prevent problems. The supplier will then become a true partner, with all the advantages that entails for both parties. *This is purchasing's ultimate quality responsibility.*

The Finance Function

As the function responsible for the accounting and control of *costs,* finance needs to be keenly aware of the potential cost impact of quality performance deficiencies in all areas of company operation. And it must see that information and data illuminating such conditions be ambitiously pursued and utilized for cost improvement.

Cost of Quality

A crucial measurement of the effectiveness of any quality improvement effort is its effect on profits. This can't be measured directly, but cost-of-quality subsystems have been created to quantify to some extent the impact of quality, or lack of quality, on company operating costs and profitability. Although not directly related to externals like market share, internal quality improvements will, in time, almost always open the door of opportunity for revenue breakthroughs.

One way to envision the improvement potential that a cost-of-quality subsystem directly addresses is to look at a distribution of how employees spend their time—and to *realize* the obvious opportunity that it represents. You can find many different estimates of this distribution, but they will usually closely follow this conservative pattern:

- *25 percent not working*—vacation, holidays, personal leave days, work breaks, arriving late, leaving early, long lunches, conducting personal business, daydreaming, talking, and so forth.

- *40 percent doing work that matters*—working on the right things, in the right order, at the right speed, at the right time, and doing it right every time.

- *35 percent redoing work*—making mistakes, confirming them, and fixing them; waiting for acceptable supplies, equipment repair, or direction for the next assignment; dealing with customer complaints or output returned; responding to problem investigations and additional data-gathering interruptions; working on the wrong thing; and other preventable activities.

Cost-of-quality systems focus on this last 35 percent, the portion that offers management the best opportunity for improvement and over which they should be able to exercise considerable control. If you doubt that this much wasted work is available for the improvement effort, choose your own percentage—what you honestly think it to be. In all studies of this distribution, the size of the opportunity has always been big.

As working systems, cost-of-quality programs were formulated many years ago to help manufacturing company quality managers get other company managers to more fully understand and accept product quality control systems strictly on the basis of profit and loss. This was accomplished through the identification and measurement of major portions of operating costs and then directly relating these measures to product quality and performance results.

Typical of the manufacturing situations encountered in the pursuit of cost-of-quality programs are the following:

- In one sophisticated electronics manufacturing plant, assembly rework costs were normally budgeted as 10 percent of overall assembly costs. A quality-cost-sponsored evaluation disclosed that the real rework costs were closer to 30 percent than to 10 percent, a condition that immediately provided credence for the start of quality-cost reporting. It's not inconceivable that the rework rate had actually been 10 percent at some point, but that must have been a long time ago.

- A components company susceptible to frequently changing marketplace demand had become greatly dependent on a number of key suppliers who were capable of handling the company's ever-changing peak production demands. Over the years, in an apparent attempt to maintain this backup position without completely resolving the accumulating problems, the company ultimately had to tolerate and work around lot rejection rates of 15 to 18 percent. Considering that hundreds of lots were received each day, this condition was obviously costly. Not so obvious, however, a large part of the real cost did not involve the rejections themselves. It involved the very challenging, day-to-day, hour-to-hour rescheduling of all production machinery affected by the rejections.

A large permanent staff of people was required for the constant movement and rescheduling of work-in-process materials—in itself the cause of other costly problems. But later, when company management made a serious commitment to vendor quality improvement and quality cost analyses, the people who turned out to be the happiest were those in the material control department. They later named themselves "The Quality Boosters."

- In this same components company, some time after management enacted the quality-cost program, the primary focus turned to in-house rework and scrap. It was suggested that each foreman be held accountable for the scrap and rework costs occurring in his or her area of responsibility. In a predictable manner, the director of manufacturing reacted as follows: "How can the foreman be held accountable for unskilled and untrained employees, inadequately maintained machinery, less-than-satisfactory materials supplied, unavailable engineering support, paperwork errors, et cetera, et cetera?"

The obvious response to any situation like this is, "How long will the manufacturing department and the company continue to tolerate such unacceptable conditions before going out of business?" *This is exactly what the cost-of-quality system is designed to expose.*

Conceptually, the philosophy of quality cost focuses on the opportunities represented by all failures to perform up to the limits of existing capabilities. It can be applied to all business operations. In general, quality costs exist as follows:

> That portion of business expenses (labor and materials) caused by "inadequate conformance to required performance standards." That is, costs resulting from customer rejections and complaints, and costs incurred due to internal errors or substandard performance causing additional work, redoing of completed work, or lost time.

As thus depicted, quality costs cannot be totally measured directly—some or all of these costs are lost somewhere in the accepted cost of doing business. Therefore, a company's quality cost system can, at best, provide an organized but indirect means of identification. Theoretically, the challenge is to measure the difference between optimum or perfect performance and actual performance. This difference is then identified as the cost of quality and targeted for reduction.

One way to look at this practice is to consider each element of the established operations budget as being made up of two parts (see Figure 2–2). The part called *ideal costs* is what the budget would be if all the work could be performed perfectly. The part represented by the difference between the ideal costs and the *actual operating costs* identifies the opportunity for cost improvement. It is referred to as the *quality variance.*

Establishing the quality variance as a measure of the difference between an ideal operations budget and actual operating costs does not imply that the business can be run perfectly. Rather, it recognizes that operating budgets, most of which

FIGURE 2–2
Quality Cost Concepts

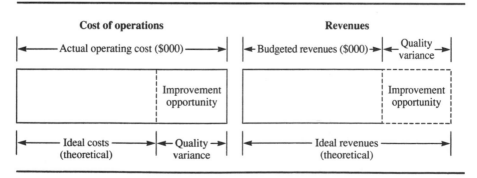

are based more on recent past history than on the true performance potential that exists, are generally lacking in any real motivation to improve. The quality variance exposes this condition for what it is—essentially an acceptance of the status quo—by emphasizing the true potential for improvement that does exist. It is then used to focus attention on and provide financial support in the pursuit of identified quality and cost improvement opportunities.

When this operations logic is understood, it can then be projected into the revenue end of the business. This is done by comparing budgeted or expected revenues with ideal revenues, which can be projected from the original sales forecasts and an analysis of their makeup. This difference is then viewed as the revenues quality variance and used to focus attention on and challenge the reasons for all short falls from these sales projections, often the result of poor quality performance. The least that can be expected to happen is that actual sales forecasting will be forced to get better—an improvement that the production planners will especially value.

In a practical manner, a quality-cost system can avail a company to examine current opportunities for cost reductions and revenue enhancements that might otherwise be hidden from management's view. A company should assign the responsibility for implementation of such a system to the finance function—that is, if that function is normally accountable for more than bean counting. Key outputs should be incorporated appropriately into financial reports. In fact, finance should take the lead in never letting the measurable cost of gross performance failures, such as excess waste and rework costs, become lost or remain hidden within other measured costs. Instead, these failures, with others to follow, need to be clearly exposed as the opportunity for cost and quality improvement they truly are.[3]

The total of the avoidable costs is the gold in the mine, *a very important fact.*
                                                                    J. M. Juran

Other Functions

The specific functions previously discussed for quality responsibilities (marketing, development, production, purchasing, and finance) were selected on the basis of their relative importance to a company. Every business entity requires the essence of these quality responsibilities in the conduct of their business. We could go on with other important functions, but it should be evident now that each identified and clearly defined business function will have some impact on overall company quality results. All that remains to be done is to examine their individual roles as they relate to the company quality mission.

Working from functional flowcharts and mission statements, all other company functions need to seek out and identify the key quality results for which they are responsible—and which have the potential to cause an unwanted, negative impact on the current and future business of the company. Each of these functions should then place their stake in the ground regarding these key functional quality responsibilities.

> *Come, give us a taste of your quality.*

Shakespeare

SUMMARY

Specific customer-oriented requirements that are established for a company's offered product or service and then translated back into each contributing function's work responsibilities are identified as the technical quality requirements of the company's product or service. They are different from the routine, day-to-day performance quality requirements applied to all employees.

As seen in Figure 2–3, technical requirements relate to "doing the right thing" *for the customer*; performance requirements (discussed in detail in Part 2) relate to "doing things right" *for the company*. Both areas of requirements provide unique opportunities for improvement.

FIGURE 2–3
From Quality Responsibilities to Quality Improvement

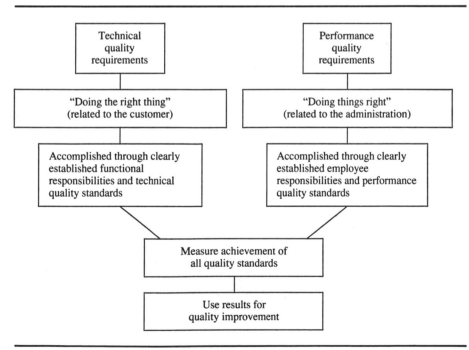

Fundamentally, technical quality requirements can be distributed into four distinct areas:

1. Marketing quality requirements—The marketing function is responsible for the quality of the marketing specification. That is, the function is responsible for clearly identifying and documenting the expectations of the end customer in technical terms most applicable to the involved business and in sufficient detail to support the product or service development process.

2. Development quality requirements—The organization or function with the assignment to convert the marketing specification into specific, usable criteria for detailed production planning and execution is responsible for the quality of design of each new offering. That is, the function is responsible for the quality of the translation from customer/sales criteria into the language of operations equipment, production and support processes, supplies, and work instructions— in other words, everything needed to prepare for production.

3. Production quality requirements—The production operations organization is ultimately responsible for the quality of the product or service as prepared and delivered to the customer. That is, the function is responsible for conformance to the specific criteria established by the product/service design or formal definition.

4. Support quality requirements—All support groups, production support and business support, are responsible for the quality of their support products or service as they pertain to marketing, development, or production technical quality requirements.

By building into the beginning of the company's quality improvement program a clear and proper distribution of functional quality responsibilities, management will have laid an important foundation for the work effort ahead. Only then will management be free to pursue companywide quality improvement and to seek the subsequent standards of people performance needed to become a quality-leader company. Unless the element of *quality* is built into all company functions from the first concept of a new product or service to the ultimate satisfaction of its users, all of which may take years to accomplish, a company cannot be confident about the actual customer satisfaction that will be achieved.

In addition, when all functions understand and fully accept their individually important responsibilities for quality, the entire concept of quality improvement begins to take on a new meaning. In a dynamic transformation from dealing with quality matters as a distraction from "more important matters," key groups within the company will be able to interact in quality improvement matters more openly and objectively—and without the built-in defense mechanisms that would otherwise be the norm. They would also begin to see quality as a valuable business asset. *Quality* will mean:

Confidence in the marketplace .... to marketing.

Challenge of a superior product or service .... to development.

Conformance and consistency .... to production.

Long-awaited opportunity .... to quality.

Investment with a guaranteed return .... to management.

Satisfaction and company quality image .... to customers.

Reputation and profitability .... to the company.

CHAPTER 3

THE CRITICAL ROLE OF HUMAN RELATIONS[1]

Another stage in the evolution of CWQI systems in America involves the understanding of human relations and its integration into the core of quality improvement systems. Lack of human relations expertise is often a stumbling block in the development and implementation of quality programs. The nature of this deterrent is depicted in the following three subsections, which deal with human relations in management, the work force, and conflict.

COMMON PITFALLS FOR MANAGEMENT

Several years of investigating companywide quality programs has shown that the perceived and promoted results of a quality program often differ from what is uncovered by digging into the real experiences of people working within the system, observes Roland A. Dumas.[2] All too often, a program is started and then discarded in favor of another program. This is most apt to happen when the company adopts the program of a particular "guru," with its prescribed bias toward a single tool. When this program does not achieve the desired outcome, the company replaces it with one of another guru, and so forth. In the end, there is a lot of unsatisfactory experience, a lot of costs, and a growing frustration with the elusiveness of genuine quality improvement.

The typical organization goes through a series of efforts that, while correct on the surface, often betray faulty assumptions or poor integration with other company efforts. Executives, for example, tend to interpret their quality problem as a worker motivation problem. They see it as a poor work ethic, a union issue, a lack of attention, or some other implied shortcomings of frontline employees. The organization then progresses through a series of programs based on the assumption that the company's quality problems are the fault of one group or another.

This faulty thinking on the part of many executives, despite their public statements to the contrary, becomes obvious through their behavior. They really believe the way to solve quality problems is to change a particular group of people. Initially, the quality focus is on the workers: motivate them, train them, reward them, regroup them, and then, in frustration, replace them with machines. Next, executives place the supervisors and middle managers under similar scrutiny.

The second wave in the quality effort generally involves tightening management controls and pushing the problems upstream to suppliers. In some cases, companies have spun off operations that had intractable quality problems and then held the new owners accountable to higher quality standards.

While there is nothing inherently wrong with any of the methods or programs companies attempt, they will not work if done in a fragmented fashion, without commitment or integration, or if attempted for the wrong reasons. Rather than being part of a larger effort to shape a new philosophy, they may appear to be part of a witch-hunt in which upper management is determined to find, and then fix or eliminate, the offending parties.

In this kind of environment, the target populations tend to resist rather than welcome the attempted improvements. For example, manufacturing managers may obey the "letter of the law" in installing statistical quality control (SQC) systems but not use the results in making decisions, preventing maintenance breakdowns, or scheduling tool replacements. The data are simply recorded and stored. Passive acceptance, pocket vetoes, and other resistance methods are also common.

On the other hand, the real situation is probably not as bleak as it might seem. As companies travel through whatever serial programs they become involved with, they are not just trying and discarding fads; it's really a learning process. Through the process of elimination, the problem eventually comes home as a leadership issue. In other words, over the long term a clear understanding evolves that systems must be integrated and led to be successful.

Most quality programs are brought in from outside sources or are adapted from packaged programs already in widespread use. Two common gaps appear in many of these programs:

1. The management-oriented programs suffer from excess awareness building and expectation raising, without adequate skill building or support. There are lots of events, meetings, affirmations, rules, and bureaucracies, but little connection to daily life on the job.

2. The engineering-oriented programs have technical methods and skills that are up to the job but cannot capture the attention of nontechnical employees, including managers. The intensely logical methods that technical professionals are used to, and prefer, tend to be deadly for others.

But the larger problem that plagues most total quality efforts is the absence of a realistic implementation plan. Some packaged systems come with a list of steps. The inference is that if all the steps are accomplished, quality will be improved. This generates a false sense of accomplishment as organizations race to get to the bottom of the list as quickly as possible, with each step taken as more of a procedure or an event to be staged.

Marketed quality programs, in general, lack the methodology for ensuring that systems, culture, skills, and other important variables are developed sensibly and effectively. The improvement process is a genuinely profound organizational change—not a corporate chain letter. It needs thoughtful, competent leadership and planning, complete with a voice strong enough to call senior managers to task for their own behavior.

The resultant major gap in most programs—integration of program requirements with technology, training methods, and implementation skills—demands a key role for two types of personnel: human resource professionals and quality professionals. Organizational development and training skills are the hallmark of a competent human resource professional. The ability to identify the technical system and technical skills required for a given job are second nature to quality professionals.

The leadership of U.S. quality programs seems to have followed an ironic evolutionary process. The origins of the typical program are found in executive initiative, the purchase of a packaged program, or the declaration of a given emphasis. But the early stages of organizationwide efforts often excluded both human resource and quality professionals. Typically, these necessary functions were only brought in to administer the program *after* key decisions were already cast in concrete and involved personnel were already following the program outline provided by outside experts. As a result, these vital professionals generally had little opportunity to contribute until it was already time for rework.

On the road to quality improvement, it's best to let your quality and human resource professionals be your guide because, otherwise:

If you don't know where you're going, no road will get you there.

THE CRUCIAL ROLE OF PEOPLE

To illustrate the importance of integrating all employees into the quality improvement process, the following synopsis of Karen Bemowski's "People: The Only Thing That Will Make Quality Work"[3] is presented.

When P. Bruce Walker became the plant manager of Dow Chemical's aspirin facility in Midland, Michigan, in 1982, he looked on the product, 11 million pounds annually, as "something I was going to eat." With that in mind, he began an effort to make the best aspirin possible. Armed only with his personal belief that people make the difference, he embarked on a journey. Walker knew his destination, but he wasn't sure how to get there.

The first thing Walker did was to open up communications at the aspirin plant. To that end, he held biweekly meetings with employees to discuss all issues. "Usually you don't air your dirty linen in front of other functions," said Walker. "But once you have done that and you get the politics out of the way, then everyone can be oriented on the only thing left—the customer."

The biweekly meetings helped reveal some of the larger quality problems, which were then handled in the traditional manner—an engineer was assigned to work on the problem with the assistance of quality assurance personnel. At the end of nine months, Walker decided to do something more. He sent a survey to all his people, asking for suggestions on how they could make their products better. He was happy but overwhelmed with the response: over 250 suggestions, of which three quarters could be implemented, and at least half of them required no money.

"So there I was back in 1983, before Dow's overall quality revolution, sitting with 250 suggestions," Walker said. "At this point I made a break with tradition." A manager with 250 suggestions would traditionally prioritize them, select the top 25, and assign them to engineers, foremen, and supervisors to resolve. At the end of the year, the 25 would be done, and the manager could say to the employees: "Look, you put in your suggestions and we did them all." He would be looking for a pat on the back, but he wouldn't get it because the employees would say: "Yes, you did 25, but what happened to the other 225 that you did not listen to? You don't listen. So we're not going to suggest any more." Walker decided not to let this happen.

Walker and the employees learned to use a Pareto chart and how to put the suggestions into perspective in terms of the biggest effect on quality and cost. Since they now had the tools to deal with suggestions, they decided to add any suggestions that were filed during the past four years. "We figured if we had 250 suggestions, what's a few more," said Walker. "We pulled out almost another 250 things to go after."

The plant personnel were divided into eight task forces and the suggestions were divided among them. The employees were challenged to prioritize the suggestions, define the problems, collect and analyze the necessary data, find the causes of the problems, brainstorm solutions, and implement the solutions that either fix the problem or control it. Only solutions requiring a great deal of capital required consultation with management.

Once the task forces started seeing improvements, they wanted to know how much they were improving. So they learned to use run charts. Then, when they saw the deviations, they wanted to know which were "noise" and which were cause and effect. Thus, statistical process control (SPC) was introduced. The employees learned and used each tool as it was needed. The tools were never forced on them.

The successes of the task force approach were many, including improvements in the whiteness of the aspirin and the number of off-color granules. Success also began spilling over into other areas, such as costs, safety, and customer service. "We actually found ourselves on a road of continuous improvement that probably went beyond sanity, beyond that ever seen before,'' said Walker. ''But it felt so good doing it, and the more people did it, the better they felt about themselves. So we kept on improving.''

All the quality efforts taking place in the aspirin plant over these years paid off. ''The bottom line to me, and the most impressive part, is that we not only improved quality, we improved in cost, we improved in safety, we improved in almost every measurement parameter you can put on a production facility,'' said Walker. The results included almost a 50 percent improvement in attendance and a 28 percent reduction in personnel requirements: off-grade production decreased by a factor of 6; on-time shipments increased to 99.2 percent; and customer relations improved.

The improvement also paid off in another important area: employee morale. ''Their belief that they were the best aspirin producers in the world made all the difference in how they viewed themselves and how they viewed their lives,'' said Walker.

It wasn't until later that Walker realized what had happened at the aspirin plant was a *process*—not a happening or accident they had stumbled onto. He realized that what actually happened was a quality improvement process that could be implemented in any operation. ''I finally realized I can go into any operation in the United States and cut 20 percent to 25 percent of the costs and have the people love doing it,'' said Walker. And having people love their jobs is important to Walker.

''I love to see people enjoy doing whatever they do. Work should be fun. If work isn't fun, you will not get good performance. When work is fun, you not only get good performance, you have people constantly striving to do better,'' said Walker. ''Being a supervisor in an environment where everybody is trying to do better is probably one of the happiest situations you can ever get into.''

There is the recognition in this story that quality is not a singular program that you can put in place and then leave to go on to something else. It is a never-ending job. If you start to think you have arrived, that's when you should get nervous. Customers are continually changing their expectations, and these changes must be continuously checked. But throughout it all, you must never doubt that people are the basis for success. *People are more important than technology and capital investments.*

RESOLVING HUMAN RELATIONS CONFLICTS

Problems involving human nature can be just as damaging to productivity and quality as technical problems, says D. Keith Denton.[4] Conflict situations involving deep, personal attitudes and feelings are as much a part of the workday as are specifications and work processes.

Managing human relations conflicts, however, is fundamentally different from resolving technical problems. To resolve a technical issue, you focus on finding the cause of the problem. But with human relations or supervisory problems, you instead need to seek solutions without probing for the causes.

Success in managing conflicts requires undistracted control of what is being communicated, as seen in the following four-step process.

Step 1—Defuse the Win-Lose Atmosphere. The first task in managing conflict is to establish a cooperative atmosphere. This means eliminating the win-lose attitude that intensifies disagreements. This will be difficult because most people look at others' opinions as being either right or wrong. It is even more difficult if people are dominated by hostile feelings. Conflicts are nurtured by hostility and suspicion. When someone feels angry toward another on the job, the best advice is to delay any discussion until a more rational mind-set returns; emotional outbursts, above all, are to be carefully avoided.

Step 2—Create a Positive Atmosphere. There are several tools that can be used to de-emphasize the negative attitudes that often occur with interpersonal conflicts.

One such tool is to emphasize common goals that people share with each other, usually revolving around economic and productivity objectives. Reminding others of mutual goals is an effective collaboration technique. Even though it may take more time, it is always better to be as specific as possible when sharing common goals. The most effective motivational goals are always concrete and specific. Agreeing on common goals not only helps resolve present disputes, it can also help to prevent future ones.

Another tool used to create positive thinking has to do with recognizing mutually beneficial rewards for each party's collaboration. Providing a list of specific promotional, monetary, status, influence, recognition, and other rewards that are likely to occur from getting the dispute resolved will help develop and maintain an atmosphere of partnership—and this can be a powerful motivating tool. Thus, the accent must be on positive outcomes that can occur when agreements are reached.

One more technique that can be used is to stress the urgency of the task—for example, key schedule dates or the cost of delay in scrap, rework, or other expenses. Most people will procrastinate when matters do not seem urgent. There is an even greater tendency to procrastinate when difficult decisions must be made. On the other hand, if stress is placed on completing the task by a specific date, collaboration is more likely.

Step 3—Simplify the Conflict. In situations of discord, it is important to first reduce the antagonism to its simplest form. This usually means reducing the emotionally charged situation ("Who does he think he is, talking to me that way?'') down to a simple disagreement—one that can more easily be managed through a rational problem-solving approach.

One way to help reduce the emotions to a manageable level, so that the conflict can be reduced to a simple disagreement, is to listen more and talk less. In an emotional situation there is a tendency for each party to become highly self-centered and not consider the other's viewpoint. It is wise to simply reduce the amount of talking, since no real dialogue is taking place. When one party shows respect by truly listening, the other party is likely to do the same in return, thus greatly enhancing the possibility for progress.

Step 4—Resolve the Conflict.   To increase the probability of reaching a final agreement, keep four objectives in focus:

1. Get your message across to the other person in a nonthreatening manner.
2. Secure an accurate understanding of your message or suggestion.
3. Accurately understand the other person's message.
4. Use a rational approach to resolve the difference.

These dialogue and feedback steps should effectively close the cycle of identifying and resolving human relations conflicts. They will also contribute to a positive business environment.

SUMMARY

Human relations are always in a state of transition, with almost every human interaction having some effect on the performance of the individuals involved. The sum total of these human interactions and the varying states of relationships with fellow employees together provide the substance for much of the excitement, joy, and sorrow that occurs in our industrial lives. Because of this and the growing belief that people really are industry's most important asset, the business leaders of America are learning to pay more and more attention to the way employees are treated.

Any resulting transition in the betterment of relations between management and the working people will prove to be a beneficial adjunct of quality improvement. In the final analysis, treating people with the dignity they deserve as human beings is the best way to improve individual efficiencies, create an openness to change, and build genuine company loyalty.[5]

CHAPTER 4

QUALITY IMPROVEMENT APPROACHES IN THE SERVICE SECTOR[1]

Within the framework of the general trend toward CWQI systems and the focus on customers and employees, there are many possible routes to the actual achievement of quality improvement. To explore the extent of variation experienced, particularly in the service sector, let's look at some of the successful approaches that have been publicized. Something can be learned from each of these shared experiences, and it is possible that any one of them may have a special appeal or fit for a particular organizational need. The variety of approaches taken is a witness to the outreach of quality improvement in all directions. In reviewing these materials, notice the consistent influence of the basic improvement process (measurement, analysis, and corrective action) and the many embodiments of specific issues already discussed.

SERVICE COMPANY DIFFERENCES

Service businesses are not as neatly structured as manufacturing businesses. Their products are not as easily defined and specified, but their systems for developing and delivering them to the customer have the same inherent possibility for human weakness, error, and failure as any other operating system. Opportunities for improvement are, therefore, based on similar premises:

- Less-than-satisfactory service internal to an organization results in *higher operating costs*.

- Less-than-satisfactory service as delivered to the customer causes a *negative impact on revenues*.

In addition to these expected opportunities, service business managers are also prime candidates for quality improvement programs because they have such a long way to go. They are far less familiar than most manufacturing company executives with the basic principles of product quality control since there has been no equivalent exposure in the history of the service industry. Therefore when first approached, even though they can be expected to initially view investments in quality improvements as additional expenses, they are really primed to be sold on the long-term improvement opportunities that do exist.

Service businesses generally have to deal with a great many individual customers—and much of their success depends on maintaining and growing this customer base. This condition creates what's referred to as *moments of truth*,[2] experiences that occur each time a customer comes in contact with a company employee or representative. How well these moments are accomplished will determine to a great extent how customers feel about the company, considering that they are almost always experienced in an intensely personal way. Customers have an important stake in each of these situations, and they will expect to be treated properly.

When unfortunate situations occur between company employees and customers, most customers will tend to be forgiving, even when greatly inconvenienced—*if* there is someone there who acknowledges their personal needs and makes a sincere effort to set things right. The concept of managing these moments of truth with the outside customer is the very essence of service management.

In all CWQI applications, each person in the line of a direct or support process is also a customer—specifically, an internal customer, equally important in the concept of quality improvement. Internal to an organization, minimoments of truth occur each time employees serve each other. And how these moments are experienced will determine, to an important degree, how employees feel about the company. Internal customers, of course, do not have the option of selecting a new supplier when they experience unsatisfactory internal service. Instead, they lose motivation or become disenchanted with the company.

According to Carol King's "Service Quality Assurance Is Different,"[3] service businesses, in addition to performing to a technical standard, must make personal behavior and staff image important quality characteristics for company operations. The manner in which a service is performed clearly relates to the behavior of the individuals providing the service. Implicit in this behavior, and irreplaceable by technology, are human elements like warmth, assurance, response, dexterity, and reasoning.

In her convincing work, King sheds light on several important aspects of the service business.

> The quality of the human interaction has always been considered important in many service industries—hotels and restaurants come to mind—but in reality the quality of behavior is a factor in virtually every service transaction that includes human contact. Patients change physicians not because of the quality of care, but because of the bedside manner. Banks have found that the friendliness of tellers and platform officers is a factor

in retaining depositors. Airlines advertise the warmth and smiles of ticket agents and flight attendants to differentiate their service from that of their competitors.

Company image as established through the behavior patterns of its employees, is a major factor in shaping customer expectations of a service and in setting the performance standards by which customers evaluate that service. Unfulfilled expectations are a large part of customer disappointments. Thus, the image itself is a component of customer satisfaction. Managing company image means, in part, keeping expectations within the realm of the possible.

The need to customize and personalize service is normally seen as a barrier to standardization, but, to a degree, this also can be standardized. When most services are examined, they are found to have a standard core with a limited range of variations that satisfy most of the demand for customization. The range of options available depends on the service organization's particular market position and resources. The delivery of these variations is as much a part of the delivery system as its core, and service standards can be developed for each clearly defined option.

The conclusion to be reached is that end-customer satisfaction for the service industry is a different challenge than it is for manufacturing. Service industries must learn to evaluate the perceived quality of their output, and service business managers must learn to deal with intangibles such as the emotional content of customer complaints or the degree of empathy shown by an employee.

DEFINING QUALITY IN SERVICE BUSINESSES

In his article, "Defining Quality in Service Businesses," Mark B. Brown has the answers for a down-to-earth approach to the understanding and pursuit of service quality standards.[4] After stating that many people come to expect bad service because they encounter it so often, Brown goes on to identify some of the basic reasons service quality is so poor in many U.S. businesses:

- Deregulation of industries, which forces companies to cut back service in order to become or remain competitive.
- Individuals unwilling to take minimum-wage service jobs.
- Untrained or uninformed employees.
- Management's disregard for service quality.

Although these are all valid causes of poor service, the major problem is that businesses have not clearly defined the quality attributes of the service being offered. Quality factors such as courtesy and response, for example, are more difficult to specify and measure than manufactured product parameters. Within all service businesses, there are three dimensions of service quality—accomplishments, behavior, and products.

Service businesses need to measure all three dimensions of service quality. Accomplishments are usually most important. They are the total service outputs delivered to customers. Behavior is activity performed by employees that affects customer relationships. Products are the physical outputs produced as part of the service (e.g., a monthly bank account statement). All service businesses produce accomplishments and have employees whose behavior is important, but some do not have products (e.g., transportation).

In the business of service, *details* distinguish the exemplary company from the average ones. Service organizations can survive without doing a good job on the details, but they will never become an IBM, a Marriott, or a McDonald's unless they pay attention to those special "extras" that can make the difference. This starts with recognizing and defining the right details to incorporate into their service offerings, those little things that matter so much to customers. The following personal touches are examples.

- The service agent at a car dealership who remembers your name.
- The dry cleaner who sews loose buttons back on garments without additional charge.
- The clothing store that alters suits free after a customer loses weight.

Customer loyalty is much more ensured by attention to such important details than by any other factor. So it follows that defining quality requirements without knowing what customers want or care about can cause the appearance of poor service quality and inadvertently drive customers away.

Defining the right details and quality requirements in a service business involves four steps:

1. Identify the service parameters for which quality requirements must be defined (e.g., order taking and food preparation in restaurant service).
2. Identify and define quality factors for each parameter (e.g., friendliness and timeliness as factors of order taking).
3. Specify at least one index for measuring each quality factor (e.g., after being seated at a restaurant, the time it takes to be greeted by a server and to actually have your order taken.
4. Define standards/requirements for each index (e.g., greeted by server and presented with any special announcements within three minutes of being seated).

To understand the extent of the required effort, consider that some service job descriptions may have only a couple of quality factors, but with 15 or 20 indexes per factor. For example, neatness and cleanliness are two important factors for a housekeeper in preparing a room for occupancy in a hotel. Hotel chains such as Hyatt and Marriott specify more than 20 separate indexes for neatness and more than 30 for evaluating the thoroughness with which a hotel room has been cleaned.

To stop or slow down the impending impact of fast-growing competition in the service sector, quality must be defined. Carefully defining the small but critical details that are meaningful and memorable to the customer is the key to success. Service companies that are presently providing quality service have already discovered the need to define very specific quality requirements for accomplishments, behavior, and products. The process outlined in this subsection will not only help any service company to be more competitive, it will provide the foundation for an effective companywide quality improvement effort to facilitate continued progress.

Good service may bring the customer back, but memorable service always will.

A QUALITY STRATEGY FOR SERVICE ORGANIZATIONS

In "A Quality Strategy for Service Organizations," Ronald Butterfield describes a five-step process to improve quality and productivity.[5] Starting with the realization that the need to proactively manage quality and productivity is slow in coming, Butterfield warns that the following two conditions are present in the service sector:

1. Markets for services are no safer from foreign competition than are markets for manufactured products.
2. Service companies are encountering the same inattention to quality, emphasis on scale economies rather than customer concerns, and short-term financial orientation that earlier injured manufacturing companies.

In the current American business climate, service-based industries offer more opportunity for growth than product-based industries did in the past. If service industries are properly nurtured, they will grow and generate much of America's future wealth. But on the downside, if they are misunderstood, disdained, or mismanaged, the same forces that led to the decline of U.S. manufacturing stand ready to cut them to pieces.

There is a gold mine just waiting to be discovered by those service organization managers who are willing to move quality and productivity from abstract concepts to practical management disciplines. But this requires a basic change in management attitude.

The management of any company has three primary objectives:

1. To enhance customer satisfaction.
2. To strengthen competitive position.
3. To improve earnings.

These basic business objectives should guide the development of quality and productivity management systems. This may seem obvious, but far too often programs are developed in isolation, resulting in political or numbers games with no real value added. Yet managers can claim they have addressed quality and productivity issues because they can produce a report that shows all is well.

If any improvement effort lacks integrity, it will do the organization much more harm than good over the long run. Employees will never produce their best work, and their active participation will be largely lost. Integrity is paramount to the success of the improvement process.

According to Butterfield, the following five-phase quality/productivity improvement process is an effective strategy for service groups:

Phase 1—Needs Assessment: Identify potential areas for quality and productivity improvement efforts as target areas for implementation.

Phase 2—Data Gathering: Collect appropriate performance information, such as current operations reports, historical facts, and other pertinent data.

Phase 3—Analysis: Determine opportunities for action planning through the compilation and analysis of collected data.

Phase 4—Action Planning: Turn findings into recommendations for implementation.

Phase 5—Follow-up and Evaluation: Assess effectiveness of action plans and their implementation.

The foundation of any ongoing improvement process is an effective performance measurement system. The performance measurement system identifies improvement opportunities, enables realistic goal setting and constructive employee feedback, and assesses the effectiveness of the improvement effort. The key is to keep the required measurements simple enough to avoid discouragement or abuse and yet provide actionable data. The measurement system is not an end in itself. The objective is not the process or the procedure—it is *improvement.*

An effective measurement system should at least provide information on current performance, trend analyses, problem identification, management actions, people issues, and needs issues. Those in the vanguard of quality and productivity management in the service industries already have such data at their fingertips. They know that *the road to success is paved with good information.* In today's competitive market, do you dare settle for less?

QUALITY PLANNING FOR SERVICE INDUSTRIES

According to Raghu N. Kacker, service industries must plan for quality to ensure that they efficiently produce highly satisfactory services.[6] Quality control is often a prerequisite for quality improvement, but the only thing that quality control itself does is to maintain prevailing quality results. Thus the primary methods for attaining unprecedented, superior levels of quality are quality planning and quality improvement.

An effective four-step program for achieving superior levels of quality in service industries follows:

1. Produce services that satisfy customer needs and expectations.
2. Produce the required services efficiently.
3. Plan for quality control and quality improvement under operating conditions.
4. Pay special attention to features that are unique to service industries.

Step 1 in producing services that satisfy customer needs and expectations is to define those services through some form of dialogue with the customer. Once the customer's needs and expectations have been identified, they must be translated into required characteristics of the service. In manufacturing situations, product quality deployment is used to translate the list of attributes desired by the customer into a list of product characteristics. A similar approach, service quality deployment, can be used in service industries.

After the service characteristics are identified, the target value and intermediate goals for each characteristic must be established. The target value, which is the ideal state of a characteristic, is established as the ultimate goal for continuous process improvement. The intermediate goals are the incremental improvement results to be met within given periods of time under operating conditions. For a critical characteristic there are no intermediate goals, just the target value. For example, financial institutions cannot afford to make any errors in customers' account balances; therefore, the goal for account balance errors is zero.

Service characteristic goals must not optimize one characteristic at the expense of another. The goals of different characteristics need to be balanced, and this balance must agree with the customers' priorities. Process capability can then be continuously improved, and as improvement occurs, the intermediate goals can be advanced toward the target value.

Step 2, once the required services have been defined, is to develop a process that can produce them efficiently. The efficiency and effectiveness of work processes can be improved by minimizing process complexities and chronic problems and by making the process immune to inadvertent human errors. Existing processes can be improved through work sampling and flowcharting to identify the errors that are responsible for the extra steps, and then by eliminating or reducing the identified errors.

Many work processes repeat chronic errors because they are modified versions of previous processes that contained these same problems. Even newly created, one-of-a-kind processes are built on relevant experiences with similar processes. Chronic errors are pervasive and often believed to be unavoidable because most organizations have diffused responsibilities for their diagnosis and remedy.

Most process planners have no incentive to take the time to diagnose and remedy chronic errors; they are usually rewarded for developing new processes in a *timely* fashion. Process planners should, however, be given, as a part of their basic mission, the responsibility for minimizing chronic errors in existing processes. This assignment will require time, resources, and a structured approach to the diagnosis and correction of problems.

One special class of errors that can be minimized by proper planning is inadvertent human errors. Such errors normally occur randomly and are mainly caused by the human inability to concentrate continuously for a long period of time. External distractions also induce such errors. Serious cases of inadvertent errors are usually prevalent in routine, repetitive, and boring operations. And there are two countermeasures against them:

1. Creatively make the work process as immune as possible to errors, utilizing input from the workers.
2. Build in mechanisms to detect and correct errors as soon as they occur.

Step 3 focuses on the fact that a process tends to become faulty when it is not being effectively controlled and improved under operating conditions. Often, not all the difficulties that occur in the operating environment can be foreseen at the planning stage. Therefore, it is necessary to plan for control and improvement under operating conditions. But service processes are frequently not planned from the viewpoint of subsequent control and improvement. To correct this condition, an essential step in quality planning for service processes is to make them more amenable to improvement. This can be accomplished by making the actual process steps highly visible and by incorporating quality control and quality improvement practices.

A written document is needed to describe the whole process. This document is crucial when the process consists of multiple work activities and involves several people. The process description must identify all subprocesses and explain their functions and relationships, but it must never become too cumbersome or difficult to understand. A useful technical aid for describing a process is a flowchart.

Diffused ownership of work activities leads to a lack of responsibility and control. Therefore, each subprocess must have an owner. A clear description of the subprocess and its interfaces will always make it easier to establish ownership. In addition to subprocess ownership, the responsibility for ensuring that the subprocesses are properly integrated must also be given clear ownership.

To maintain acceptable quality standards during operations, deviations need to be identified and corrected. This control process consists of comparing actual performance with the standard and taking corrective actions to reduce deviations. To implement a control process, you must establish process checkpoints, where comparison with individual characteristic standards takes place, and an organized method for determining both the causes of deviations and the proper corrective actions.

The natural locations for process checking are the boundaries and the interfaces of subprocesses. At these locations you can determine the extent to which the input and output requirements are being met. Also, process checking at functional interfaces discovers deviations from the standard before they are carried over to later steps.

Major improvements for long-standing quality problems normally happen by project. For each quality improvement project, an interdepartmental project team can be organized. This team is responsible for bringing the project to a successful conclusion.

In most project team cases, the path to success consists of two journeys— a *diagnostic* journey and a *remedial* journey. The diagnostic journey begins with the precise definition of the problem and ends with the diagnosis of the root causes. The remedial journey starts with the search for effective remedies and ends with the implementation of those remedies that will attain superior quality levels under normal operating conditions.

Step 4 recognizes that although basic approaches to attaining quality improvement are common to service-producing and goods-producing industries, some aspects of service require added emphasis. Service industries, for example, must pay attention to *auxiliary* and *unobligatory* services, extra services that are provided in connection with a primary service.

Auxiliary services, such as providing an alternate means of transportation in the event of a vehicle breakdown, are expected by the customer. Failure to provide these services will result in customer dissatisfaction. Unobligatory services, such as free drinks and cookies in the waiting room, may be expected by the customer, depending on the prevailing convention. When they are provided, the customer is usually pleased.

Most manufactured products are produced in the factory and then delivered to customers, thus allowing product quality and delivery schedule to be treated separately. Services, on the other hand, are often produced after they are ordered. The waiting time to access the service and the action time to receive the service are usually regarded as integral aspects of the quality of service.

In addition, customers of service industries have a wide range of needs, expectations, and preferences, and they have wide differences in their abilities and willingness to pay for the desired services. Many service industries, therefore, provide multiple choice offerings to reach a larger number of customers.

For example, insurance companies provide complex combinations of coverages to suit the client's willingness to take different kinds of risks.

In all situations, high standards of quality and productivity in service industries are achievable *if quality is carefully planned for*. That is the message of this segment.

CREATING A CUSTOMER-CENTERED CULTURE FOR SERVICE QUALITY

According to Robin Lawton, the first challenge in service organizations is to define and seek out that which is *wanted*, not that which must be eliminated.[7] The way to do this is by first treating service as a tangible product.

A product is a thing. Tangible and countable, it occurs in discreet units. Using product-centered strategy in a service organization can be the key for creating a customer-centered culture. Creating such a culture, one responsive to both internal and external customers, can be done with a method called *total performance management* (TPM). The six steps of TPM are:

1. Define the service product.
2. Identify customer requirements.
3. Compare the product with requirements.
4. Describe the production process.
5. Measure productivity, quality, and profitability.
6. Include customers in product development.

TPM refers to both a philosophy and a system for simultaneously addressing quality, productivity, profitability, and innovation. *Step 1* is to define the service product. The product of an organization is the tangible unit that most closely represents its mission. This is always a thing, and it is often in the form of packaged information. Simple examples include invoices, reports, contracts, loans, meals, blueprints, business plans, and memos. Every product has a producer and at least one customer.

Step 2 is to identify the product's customers and to account for their separate requirements in a balanced way. Customer requirements for a product can be viewed as attributes or characteristics. They can almost always be measured. If a financial report is the service product, the requirements will include a certain level of accuracy, ease of use, timeliness, and so forth. This is the basis for quality—the degree to which the product meets the measurable requirements of its customers.

Step 3 is to measure the actual service product delivered and compare the results to established requirements. Usually one of these two conditions is discovered:

1. The product has *fewer* attributes or performs to a lower level than required.
2. The product has *more* attributes than required.

The first case represents a chance to improve quality. The second is a challenge to improve productivity, because the product is requiring more resource investment to produce it than is really necessary. This is usually the result of an overly complex product. Rarely is there a perfect match between customer requirements and the actual service product delivered, because expectations are constantly changing. That is why a customer-centered orientation is needed for the management of service quality.

Step 4 is to describe the process used to produce and deliver the service product. Since many processes in large organizations cut across several functional units, it can be hard to find an owner for the process. If there is no clear owner, there can be no easy control exerted on the process to produce what customers expect. The objective is to make any process come as close as possible to a straight line between two points. Figuratively, it should have the fewest moving parts possible.

Graphically describing the flow of service processes is an excellent way to see who is actually doing what, to identify targets of opportunity, and to reduce complexity and cost. The graphic description of a process can easily lead to an obvious conclusion, as Kaoru Ishikawa succinctly stated: "The next person in the process is your customer." This step is critical to creating a customer-oriented culture.

Step 5 is to complete the measurement picture. Financial performance is only one important area to routinely measure. An organization managing for total performance should use three types of measures on a broad basis:

1. Productivity—in terms of quantity and timeliness.
2. Quality—in terms of conformance and yield.
3. Profitability—in terms of cost and dollar value produced.

The previous five steps should provide the necessary foundation for the appropriate measures that organizations should use for every major service product. Many organizations have at least some of this information, but it is often fragmented. Organizing the data by tangible service product will provide a well-balanced view of performance and an objective basis for continuous improvement.

Step 6, the final one, is to include the customers as part of the product development team. Not only can this provide a focus for product quality and its improvement, it can also help generate new ideas. In a customer-centered culture, we ask the customers what to improve and how to do it. Their response is product oriented; it is incremental and it is often a catalyst for innovation.

Creating a customer-centered culture requires of management both a philosophical commitment and skill training for implementation. Analytical tools, and training in their use, are necessary to achieve a structured or guided approach to change. Executives and managers seeking to bring about culture changes need not embark on massive orientation and training programs. Selecting small projects in areas already receptive to change creates the successes necessary to get broader commitment to, and participation in, the change process.

Success comes from having the proper aim as well as the right ammunition.

Proverb

QUALITY PLAN DEVELOPMENT: A STEP TOWARD CUSTOMER ENTHUSIASM

According to J. Stephen Sarazen, in business in general there are operating plans, financial plans, and strategic business plans—but quality plans, truly necessary for business success, are rare.[8] The road to performance excellence begins with a quality plan.

Developing a quality plan requires a framework from which to start. The following basic model can be applied to any plan.

Phase 1—A Philosophy for Quality. This phase includes the establishment of:
  a. A vision.
  b. A clear policy.
  c. Primary quality objectives.
  d. Guidelines for meeting those objectives.

Once these are established, a company quality philosophy exists.

Phase 2—Tactics. This phase provides the ways and means for putting the philosophy into operation through:

  a. Specific programs and projects.
  b. The creation of an ongoing review process to help the business to understand its progress and make necessary adjustments when appropriate.

This basic model can be specifically adapted to a quality plan using the following eight-step process.

1. *Obtain management commitment through sponsorship.*   Most books and articles about quality talk about the importance of management commitment, which is indeed critical. The most senior manager in the organization must be firmly established as the sponsor of the quality plan development process, and a direct communications pipeline to that person must always be kept open, even if it is just for occasional sanity checks.

2. *Form the team.*   Every effort must be made to get the best and the brightest representatives from each function on the team. For best results, the team members need sound knowledge of the business they represent and should possess the attributes of integrity, communication, cooperation, innovation, and leadership. The team's mission must be clear and the members committed for the duration. The development process and implementation may take from three to six months, or longer.

3. *Develop a vision.*   What does quality success look like? How will an organization know it when it sees it? This is the vision, and any statement describing it should be short, readable, and measurable. It should be written in the present tense, as though its goal had already been achieved—for example, "XYZ Company has adopted quality as its number-one operating priority and leads the industry in customer satisfaction."

In this example, the measurement of leading the industry can be determined through an annual survey. A sampling of customers for the industry will determine whether quality is perceived as the operating priority for this company. The vision gives everyone in the organization something to shoot for, something they can share, and a way to take pride in accomplishments along the way.

4. *Develop a policy statement.*   In this step, it becomes clear whether or not senior management has made the necessary commitment, because it is management's responsibility to set policy. Management may require the help of the quality team, but in any case, the policy should be kept short and understandable at all levels of the organization. The goal is to have each individual adopt the message personally. Any person reading the policy must clearly feel its intent personally.

5. *Develop objectives and guidelines.*   In the planning model, objectives and guidelines are treated as two separate issues. In one sense, they are separate in that the objectives are clearly at a higher level. In another sense, they are closely related, because the objectives may not stand alone. Therefore, it is best to enter into this step with the team focused on the key objectives, but constantly asking what is required from the organization to achieve the objectives. It is important to listen to all input and then narrow the number of objectives and supporting guidelines down to a workable and understandable number.

By this time, the team has put a great deal of effort into the plan and there have likely been lengthy philosophical discussions. The team is stronger now and has a sound base from which to move on. Before moving to Phase 2, however, it is a good idea to review the work to date with the sponsor and the management team. Once they, in turn, have agreed that the planning team is moving in the right direction, Phase 2 can begin.

6. *Review current programs and projects.* In this step, the team reviews the vision, policy, objectives, and guidelines. The team then asks what needs to be done to achieve the vision, support the policy, meet the objectives, and internalize the whole quality philosophy. Where the organization presently stands on quality determines the work to be done.

The team now develops a list of needs and a list of programs and projects to meet the needs, including any new programs, projects, and resources that are required. All of these programs and projects must be in place before implementation, meaning that everyone involved understands and is committed to his or her individual participation.

7. *Develop and implement a formal review process.* Establishing a monitoring tool, or review process, is a key step toward ensuring that the quality plan is a living document. This can be done in several ways. One method is to have the senior staff routinely invite several of the project managers to present the program status, progress, issues, concerns, needs, and corrective actions. This provides visibility for the program and helps the staffers to show their interest by staying in touch. Another approach is to form a quality board of directors that meets routinely. This board can provide ongoing program review and assistance as required.

8. *Implement the plan.* Quality improvement is not a quick-fix solution for the company's ills but rather a permanent "way of life." Recognizing this can help the organization avoid rushing into a quick and possibly false start. Taking the time to carefully prepare people for their lifetime involvement in the improvement program is what's called for—and this crucial investment will guarantee long-term results. Careful preparation for implementation will build on the importance the organization is placing on quality, encourage managers to communicate with their people, provide a forum for idea generation, and get people behind the common vision.

The development of a quality plan is a complex undertaking. Once started with that first planning step, a company needs to make sure that all subsequent quality plans complement one another, thus providing a sound basis for the continued pursuit of excellence and customer enthusiasm. Concurrently, the plan will have a better chance to succeed if all business partners are committed to its success and the team sticks to the following guidelines:

- Plan it right—keep it short and simple.
- Make it fun—be innovative.
- Implement it—involve everyone.
- Monitor it—show results.
- Make it last—stress *continuous* improvement.
- Make it rewarding—recognize excellence.
- Sustain its success—focus on customer enthusiasm.

SUMMARY

This modern view of managing a service company—knowing the quality differences, becoming customer oriented, promoting quality planning, measuring quality performance, focusing on work processes, utilizing quality teams, and implementing a formal review process—is a composite of ways to become and remain truly competitive in this fastest growing segment of American industry. No matter what position you may currently occupy in the marketplace you serve, any part of this general approach is guaranteed to help improve your position.[9]

PART 1—CONCLUSION

This decade of quality improvement transition has been composed of four distinct but interrelated strategic approaches:

1. A transition of entrepreneurial ideas challenging individual functional organizations to recognize and grasp the opportunities for constructive change being offered by the quality improvement movement.
2. A transition of business understanding and the clear assignment of organizational responsibilities for quality.
3. A transition in the recognition and acceptance of the true value of working people and in the way in which they are treated.
4. A transition in the recognition and growing value of quality improvement as an integral part of effective management.

In reading between the lines, you can easily detect a few underlying rules of conduct that greatly enhance whatever path is chosen:

- Take care of the basics—prepare people for change.
- Combine system changes with social change—within the company.
- Focus on concepts—relate them to people's jobs.
- Concentrate on value—there is no higher standard.

Before concluding our discussion of the transitions of the eighties, take time to read the following brief reprint from *Industry Week Magazine*. It is a prime, must-read, down-to-earth example of one company's quality experience—a story of sincerity, innovation, generosity, and huge success.

QUALITY COW GIVES FREE MILK
Maybe There *Is* Such a Thing as a Free Lunch

Usually when something is free, it's fattening, clogs the arteries, has been linked to cancer, or really does end up costing the recipient money.

The often-repeated business adage that there are no free lunches couldn't be proved by the results of a central-Wisconsin company's quality/participation program. It has the numbers to disprove the adage. Employees have a new sense of self-esteem, along with special bonuses in their pockets. And all short-term debt has vanished from the balance sheets of Modern of Marshfield, Inc.

The $6 million Marshfield, Wis., custom sofa/sleeper-maker and its 100 employees have never been so prosperous in a flat sales year, mostly because of a quality program started in September 1988.

"I attribute 80% to 90% of our results to our quality program and the combined efforts of all of our employees," observes William J. Mork, president. "Even though our sales were level or slightly down for our fiscal year ended July 31, 1989, our profitability was up."

Each employee received a bonus—with the total equaling 25% to 33% of fiscal-year profits—at a tribute luncheon on October 25. It was the first time employees were given a bonus in other than a boom year in sales or profits.

Here are some of the sudden, though not pain-free, results of the quality/participation program:

- Modern's cash position improved 232% from fiscal 1988 to fiscal 1989.
- Receivables were down 40%—the company got paid faster for its finished products because quality was up and disputes were down.
- Inventory fell 40%.
- Current liabilities dropped 51%.
- Long-term liabilities declined 25%.
- Total liabilities were reduced 42%.
- Debt-to-equity ratio before the quality program was 1.8 to 1. It's now 0.9 to 1 in an industry where the median debt-to-equity ratio is 1.5 to 1. For every $100,000 worth of debt, the company now has $110,000 worth of equity. Previously, the company had just $55,000 in equity for every $100,000 worth of debt.
- Total company assets thus far have been reduced 26%.

We're not just liquidating our assets to gain an improvement in our profits," Mr. Mork says. "We're turning our assets better. Fabric is a key element [vulnerable to obsolescence]. We used to turn that inventory three to four times a year; now we turn it six times a year.

Quality Cow *(continued)*

"We have reduced our fabric inventory 50% without creating any shortages, and our customers' needs are better satisfied than ever," stresses Mr. Mork, who claims his working title is actually dependent upon who shows up for work.

"Our program also generated the necessary cash to retire all of our short-term debt and a portion of our long-term debt. Our banker thought we must have switched financial institutions when we paid off all of our loans due in less than one year," laughs Mr. Mork.

It wasn't Mr. Mork's intention to embrace "quality religion" solely for its economic benefits. Instead, he reasons, "we just wanted to be a better company in the eyes of our customers and colleagues."

The real cornerstone of the company's quality/participation program was a change in the corporate culture and in management's attitude. Rather than management by demigods, Mr. Mork reveals, Modern's philosophy of management is: "You [employees] talk; we [management] will listen—and together we'll act."

The company also pushed decision-making down to its most practical and effective level. An example is the change in duties and responsibilities for Kurt Frome, who formerly was in charge of receiving, inventorying, and distributing foam products where needed in the plant. Now, in addition to those tasks, Mr. Frome is responsible for buying the foam, ensuring its quality level when it arrives at the plant, and scheduling its delivery date.

"He's now vice president in charge of foam," jokes Mr. Mork.

In order to prepare Mr. Frome for his new duties, "all we had to do was give him the authority to do it and the information on how we cost the foam we purchase," Mr. Mork says with a shrug.

The furniture maker also implemented an employee-suggestion program called Modern of Marshfield's Program of Participation, or Mom's and Pop. Employee suggestions for improving quality are all responded to within 48 hours. If company dollars are actually saved through a new procedure, the sponsoring employee gets a lump-sum cash payment equal to 10% of the cost reduction, and a second 10% of the savings is placed in a special fund for eventual distribution to employees.

At any given time there are about a dozen quality teams, called CATS, or corrective-action teams, at work on improvement efforts until they either achieve success or reach an impasse, at which point, in either case, they are disbanded. A QIT, or quality-improvement team, oversees the work and progress of all CATS and also reviews all employee suggestions.

The QIT is comprised of six colleagues of the month, each of whom has earned the position through his or her quality-improvement efforts. (Each col-

---

Quality Cow (concluded)

league of the month gets a special 30-day company perk: the only reserved parking space on the premises. In addition, the colleague of the year wins an all-expense-paid vacation.)

"Our past problems with quality weren't because employees wanted to make bad products," observes Mr. Mork. Rather, "we as management failed to define what constitutes a good quality product. It's our responsibility to define that."

The corporate-culture change and the stress and strain of improving quality at Modern haven't been an easy uphill climb. "It's been more like a roller-coaster ride," the president comments. "It's a big change when you move from a system in which management has all the control to where you share power and control with employees.

"In this kind of system, policies and procedures need to be flexible, and guidelines for how we run our business can't be refuges for inaction like our old bureaucratic suggestion system.

"Our success to date doesn't mean that we have by any stretch of the imagination made a complete conversion in our company, but there is a new direction now. We've just taken a few steps, and many more steps are ahead of us," Mr. Mork says.

Source: Brian S. Moskal, *Industry Week,* March 19, 1990, pp. 27, 30. Reprinted by permission.

During this decade of transition, a growing number of manufacturing and service companies embarked on a variety of journeys into the realm of quality improvement. Some have gone on to great heights. Others have fallen by the wayside or are still struggling to reach a higher plateau. The problems encountered were not necessarily caused by the assortment of approaches available. Rather, they mostly had to do with the deep-down conversion of management and staff support functions to the openness, honesty, and discipline required to experience genuine quality progress.

Something important seems to be missing in these less-than-satisfactory scenarios. Managements, under pressure from the competition, seem to be willing to grasp at whatever brass ring looks interesting or profitable at the moment; they take a decidedly narrow view of the *big picture* of quality improvement. That's why programs get started before companies are ready and why there isn't a broader and deeper pattern of success. Managements are too ready to focus on the payoffs at the end of the journey and not on the journey itself, which contains all the real value.

As world competition continues to mount in all areas of business, U.S. service and manufacturing businesses should take heed of the inherent competitive value of long-term process performance improvements. A great unexploited opportunity exists today for its accomplishment. All that's needed for a company to begin reaping these benefits is for it to look beyond price competition and quick fixes and to focus seriously on the long-term quality, schedule, and cost opportunities presented in this discussion. That's the price of entry into the world of quality competition, a world without letup.

Only you can determine what is the right path to quality improvement for your company. In all likelihood, it will entail ideas from the areas we've discussed. But to help you with the far-reaching effects of this decision, let's now look at where we want to be when we get there.

PART 2

QUALITY MANAGEMENT TOMORROW: THE IDEAL MANAGEMENT SYSTEM

In this part you will be introduced to everybody's ultimate quality program: total quality management (TQM). You'll examine what it consists of and determine for yourself whether it is:

    a. The quality professional's dream-come-true.

    b. The CEO's latest hope for survival in a quality-driven marketplace.

    c. A genuine chance for continuous quality progress.

    d. All three of the above.

Next, you will explore in depth the central idea of the ongoing quest for quality progress and start to delve into the substance of how managers manage. Here you will consider the interactions of conventional business practices and their impact on quality performance.

This "central idea" is followed by a detailed examination of the principles that make up the deeper meaning of TQM and how it must affect the people who will make it work—that is, all employees. This overall guideline is basically a detailed roadmap for traveling the path of continuous quality improvement. It is the way to truly *integrate* quality into the people and the management system of the company—an organized way to do what Japanese managements accomplished more *naturally* when they became "sold on" and totally committed to quality.

Finally, the question of where all this is leading to is answered—the "payoff" at the end of the road is *management excellence.*

CHAPTER 5

TOTAL QUALITY MANAGEMENT—THE ULTIMATE ADAGE FOR QUALITY

While many fundamental, and still effective, quality improvement programs continue to be promoted, most of what has been happening in industrial quality programs for the past several years is being accumulated and discussed under the banner of *total quality management* (TQM). This term has come to imply the ultimate achievement possible in the pursuit of quality improvement for all of industry, and that it can be accomplished at a revolutionary rate of progress.

In its simplest form, TQM means "total integration of the *continuous improvement process* into all work." The most visible evidence of this comes from the U.S. Department of Defense, which has made TQM its key strategy in effecting permanent changes in how jobs get done by defense contractors.[1] But this initial government effort is progressively being outdone by a growing awareness and acceptance of TQM in the broadest possible segment of product and service companies.

Although TQM theoretically includes all known tools and methodologies of successful quality improvement programs, it has become a catchall for any combination of quality tools and strategies that someone may choose to propose or write about. This is evidenced by a steady outpouring of publications seeking to define the true concept.

TQM is regularly found as a current topic in local and national newspapers, magazines, journals, and books of every variety. But what you find may be just a small piece of the action, or it may simply be a hodgepodge of quality ideas being promoted or, in the worst case, exploited. You, the potential user, will have to determine whether you've discovered the keys to the kingdom of quality treasures or just another fantasy.

CONTINUOUS QUALITY IMPROVEMENT

The underlying theme of most discussions of TQM is twofold: (1) the need for sufficient cultural changes in industry to support the concept of continuous quality

FIGURE 5–1
Total Quality Management

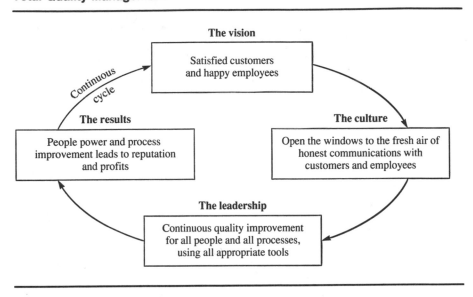

improvement, and (2) the need to carry this concept beyond traditional quality assurance applications into *all* work processes, ultimately including management. Figure 5–1 illustrates a closed-loop notion of this underlying theme.

TQM's basic strategy is to integrate primary management techniques, existing improvement efforts, and technical tools into a disciplined approach focusing on how to improve the way work is actually getting done. It directly addresses customer satisfaction, elimination of chronic waste, and reduction of excess variability in performance.

You might say the secret of TQM is that it provides the means for a company to get all its component parts working energetically and in unity by using the *best knowledge available* about the how-to's. This is opposed to a company's future more or less resting on the shoulders of a few key executives and their leadership abilities. No matter how good these key company executives are, and many of them are truly outstanding, they could never collectively compete with *the total company machinery working up to its full capability*.

In its extreme state, company culture is permeated by an atmosphere of mistrust, with intricate checks and balances applied by a mind-boggling bureaucracy attempting to control important actions. This is the chief cause of excessive administrative costs. Meanwhile, managers are not trained for leadership, pay little attention to a system that allows counterproductive efforts to go unchallenged, and do not properly educate, train, or motivate subordinates to be effective and productive.

Under these conditions, the cultural changes required are rather obvious. What's needed is an open management environment and a participative working climate in which the improvement process can take hold and flourish. Management will discover, if the process follows the norm, that its major accomplishments are firmly rooted in ethical behavior, customer satisfaction, and longterm strategy success.

The details of TQM strategy, once the company culture has been opened up, revolve around employees and customers. No one is left out. All work functions—production operations and white-collar endeavors—generate output. That means work processes have to exist, and *processes can be improved.* The full potential for improvement, inherent within the work force, will be tapped when each employee receives proper training, obtains feedback on performance, and is *empowered* to make changes that will improve the process.

Coupled with employees and functions are the tools of TQM, which are always promoted as an integral part of the total effort. First you'll find the common, routine tools of all improvement efforts; these include cause and effect diagrams, Pareto charts, histograms, check sheets, input/output analyses, scatter diagrams, and work flow analyses. Next, and most important, are the revitalized statistical standards like design of experiments, statistical process controls, and control charts; these are followed closely by other, more recent standards like concurrent engineering, cost-of-quality, and just-in-time material control techniques. Finally, you can expect to be directed towards current, breakthrough tools like quality function deployment, benchmarking, and Taguchi methods for robust design. The tools are there and they work. The Japanese have proved that.

Customer satisfaction is the goal for which everyone must strive, whether the customer is internal or external. *Customer* and *user* are generic terms for the recipient or beneficiary of a process's output—that is, its resultant product or service. The user is satisfied only if the product or service meets his or her needs. Therefore, knowledge of the user's needs and expectations has to become a routine, built-in requirement of all work processes.

It is typical for any discussion of TQM to include a structure or model for implementation of the continuous quality improvement process. This generally comprises some combination of the following key elements:

1. Establish the desired cultural environment, or at least open the management windows to let in the fresh air of ethical behavior, customer-first thinking, employee dignity, and long-term business strategies.

2. Affirm or reestablish a clear definition of responsibilities and mission for each segment of organization.

3. Measure work-process outputs to determine the level of individual or

group performance and achievement of technical quality requirements. Correct the obvious problems, and establish improvement goals for all areas.

4. As applicable, organize specific improvement projects, corrective action teams, self-directed process improvement teams, and other major action plans.

5. Implement standard improvement procedures in consonance with the start of major improvement projects, utilizing applicable quality improvement tools and methodologies.

6. Maintain ongoing measurement, evaluation, and reporting as essential ingredients of the improvement process to confirm progress and support continued efforts.

The difference between TQM and traditional quality improvement programs is that TQM encompasses every aspect of quality management that has been thought of to date. That's the claim you find firmly entrenched, or at least implied, in every TQM text or program. TQM is universal. It is the final answer on the question of quality.

Although TQM is a good idea, there are weaknesses to be found in any single TQM description or program. The reason is that management excellence, TQM's ultimate underlying objective, is not a commodity that can be bought and sold. Rather, it is a deliberately thought-out, slowly evolving, unique achievement that, at best, is either motivated or strongly influenced and guided by individual concepts of TQM.

It is now generally accepted that poor quality and poor overall performance is at least 80 percent the result of the process and not the employee, and the process is the responsibility of management. But the transformation in management culture and leadership required to attack this condition is a long, slow, arduous journey, often in uncharted waters. During the early days of this journey, management will come to realize what has become a consensus impression of the TQM experts. That is, TQM means management of four basic pillars of business:

- *Customer.* Management must become customer-driven, for both the *external* and the *internal* customer. This means anticipating and meeting or exceeding the customers' needs and desires.

- *Quality.* With *quality* being "as defined by the customer," it must become the number-one priority of the enterprise, taking precedence over *all* other considerations, specifically over cost and schedule.

- *Continuous process improvement.* Lasting improvement can only be obtained by focusing on the process that produces the results rather than on the results alone. And, since customers' expectations will continue to rise, the need for continuous process improvement must, therefore, be anticipated and continuously enacted.

- *People.* These are the most important part of any process. Unless employees can learn to have a common vision of success, share common goals, work as a team, and devote their minds and energies to their work achievements, the enterprise will fail.

SUMMARY

It can be said that TQM is a postgraduate course for the students of quality improvement; it triggers lots of actions, mostly good but some that could only be categorized as noisy gongs and clanging cymbals. It is well intended and universally useful, in the sense that any attempt to achieve TQM will help executives and managers to concentrate on and appreciate the business value of quality improvement.

At the very least, TQM is replete with good tools and ideas, many of which can be specifically useful and productive for various segments of a business or industry. However, you should review more than one article, one program, or one expert's opinion. Consider many different approaches before deciding what best fits the needs of your unique situation. But, by all means, learn all you can and do something. The more you know before you start, the better.

I find the great thing in this world is not so much where we stand, as in what direction we are moving: To reach the port of heaven we must sail sometimes with the wind and sometimes against it—but we must sail, and not drift, not lie at anchor.

Oliver Wendell Holmes

Now, after picturing TQM in its proper perspective, let's explore a deeper view of how quality improvement fits into the overall concept of running a business.

CHAPTER 6

THE CENTRAL IDEA OF
QUALITY IMPROVEMENT

Over the past two decades, there has been an explosion of communications about quality improvement for both manufacturing and service companies and, most recently, about total quality management and its growing reputation. A lot of information and promotion exists; but there's not nearly enough proven experience in practical, ongoing, quality improvement systems with well-documented results.

Many "quality" advocates talk about "how good it's going to be," but not enough about "how good it is right now." A major part of this difficulty can be attributed to the situations and challenges discussed in Part 1—obstacles that need to be identified and addressed before companies are ready to move forward. Another part of the problem is in learning that quality is not free; it takes investment, commitment, participation, and being open to change in the way the business is managed. The balance of the problem lies in the design and implementation of the quality improvement system itself.

Not all CWQI or TQM systems are alike. Most system designers or quality experts are individualists. While they may all believe in the same basic principles and in the need to involve all employees, their actual approach to quality improvement is distinctive to their individual thinking. And while all approaches may have merit, they are not equal—especially as they might pertain to a particular company's needs. Each company, therefore, must attempt to understand the deeper meaning of quality improvement and specifically apply this knowledge to its own planning and commitment.

PERSONAL RESPONSIBILITY FOR QUALITY

In Chapter 2, we discussed the understanding and incorporation of organizational quality responsibilities as the means for establishing the technical quality standards required by each involved function. Now, before proceeding with a discussion of the central idea of quality improvement, let's look at the other side of the responsibility coin, a general distribution of *people* quality responsibilities dispersed throughout different levels of organization. (Refer to Figure 2–3, "From Quality Responsibilities to Quality Improvement," on page 39.)

When personal quality performance is viewed as conformance to a job standard—a standard that includes applicable technical quality requirements—it should be easy to envision that the achievement of *overall* quality performance depends on each and every employee, from executive to operator, performing up to the individual standards for his or her job. This thesis strongly reinforces the need for quality improvement to be a companywide endeavor. A break in this human chain of quality work in any one place will always affect the quality of the end results (see Figure 6–1).

When a worker is hired to do a job, it is normally agreed what he or she is expected to do. Generally speaking, employees are either unskilled or they bring a particular knowledge, skill, or profession to be adapted to the company's

FIGURE 6–1
Quality Responsibility

unique system of operations. All too often, however, when personal quality responsibilities are not clearly and firmly established at the start of employment, a new hire will take only about two or three days to learn that a small error rate is customarily tolerated.

New hires learn very quickly what kind of conduct is allowable and what limits of performance are acceptable. In this way they are able to quickly adapt to, and not disrupt, the norm. In essence, they are conforming to the actual quality performance standard that currently exists for the area in which they have been hired, rather than finding the responsibility for quality to be a condition of employment as natural as getting to work on time.

Establishing an exact quality performance responsibility for each new hire simply means honestly telling them that they are not expected to make errors or to shirk their basic responsibilities and duties in any way whatsoever. Make it clear to them that follow-up actions will be taken to ensure this vital personal responsibility for quality. *You can't have it both ways.*

If the individual hired cannot perform the functions necessary to meet the job specification, management must take remedial action. Failure to take remedial action when it becomes clear that the wrong person was hired to do a job is a worst-case scenario for quality. It is impossible to achieve quality progress under such circumstances because an unbusinesslike level of toleration has become the de facto company quality performance standard.

A comforting side of this management follow-up responsibility, however, is that most prospective employees do understand and are willing to accept a personal responsibility for quality. They know, from their own personal experiences with doctors, dentists, bankers, airline pilots, pharmacists, and others, what would happen if errors were routinely tolerated. In fact, when employers do *not* demand this same personal standard of performance, most new employees become somewhat "demotivated" before they ever really get started, a condition that cries out for formal quality improvement.

In addition to the same performance demands applied to workers for those basic duties they are entrusted with, supervisors need to be charged with fundamental quality management responsibilities. That is, they are to be held accountable for managing the quality of all work performed in their assigned area, no different than managing cost and schedule. This includes individual quality performance as well as the overall quality results as affected by any combination of workers, tools, equipment, supplies, instructions, training, and so forth.

To accomplish this administrative responsibility, supervisors must know the level of quality performance being achieved, identify the current most significant contributors to less-than-perfect quality performance, and have a practical working plan for the corrective action necessary to eliminate these problems. As will be shown more clearly later, this is the hub of the quality improvement process— a microcosm of the *continuous quality improvement* introduced in the discussion of TQM.

FIGURE 6–2
Quality Improvement Responsibilities

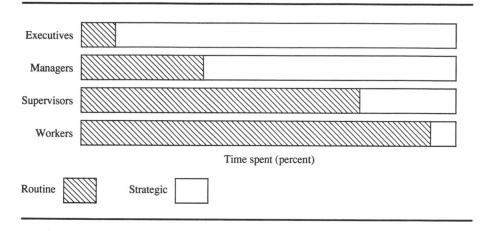

Normally, middle managers and executives are held accountable for the quality of the administrative and executive work for which they are individually assigned. But to strengthen overall quality progress companywide, these executives must take the responsibility for *monitoring, questioning, and promoting* continuous quality improvement in direct support to the supervisors' responsibility for *the management of quality.* By so doing, they will be in the proper position to recognize and act on the need for strategic quality improvement actions, such as an investment in better support tools or a major retraining effort.

These clear management responsibilities apply regardless of the particular quality improvement system to be installed. In essence, the higher the level of management the less is the need for routine quality improvement disciplines and the more is the need for creative, investment-oriented, breakthrough quality improvement ideas. Figure 6–2 illustrates a distribution of disciplines versus strategies.

The experience of the eighties has shown that a company will greatly enhance its chances for success in the pursuit of CWQI if it clearly establishes both the technical and personal responsibilities for quality at all organizational levels and for all functions *before* attempting to implement a quality improvement system. Laying this important foundation of understanding can build confidence for the work ahead.

THE CENTRAL QUALITY SYSTEM

The usual approach to quality improvement involves the direct and universal application of the continuous improvement process to all functions; but the route to be followed here is different. Essentially, it is a quality support system for the business management system already in place, with its ultimate aim being the complete integration of continuous quality improvement into the current management system. It must, therefore, be committed to in its entirety.

The key business elements, including the to-be-installed improvement process, most crucial to the practical functioning of CWQI systems are collectively presented as the *central quality system.* These individual components are linked together in synergistic combination to directly engage and support the business structure in which continuous improvement is to become a functioning, integral part.

This quality support system consists of four distinct but interrelated, individually challenging, and individually important business components: communications, education, recognition, and the improvement process. Each one of these must be fully understood, integrated, and controlled if quality improvement is to have a fighting chance (see Figure 6–3).

Figure 6–3 shows at a glance the four interrelated components of the central quality system. The *improvement process* is that unique version of the continuous improvement process the company has chosen for application to all its personnel and functions. *Communications* embodies the company work atmosphere—the degree of openness and honesty in which the improvement process must function and flourish. *Education* is the sum total of learning and training that enables all personnel to buy into and participate in quality progress. This is always a major investment issue. And *recognition* is the leading component of the sustaining power that will keep quality progress moving forward. Constructive management

FIGURE 6–3
Central Quality System

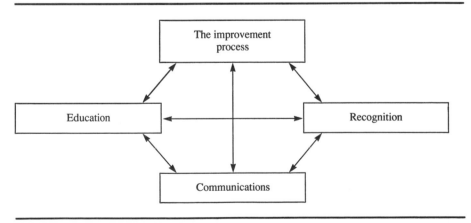

action in any of these four areas individually can contribute to improved company performance; but taken together, they form an excellent infrastructure for outstanding quality progress. Figuratively speaking, this approach is like adding an exercise program to a dieting commitment—that is, it considers the *whole* body of management thinking and not just the symptoms of its quality failures.

Communications

The delicate nature of the quality improvement process—in the sense of personally engaging each and every employee to focus on improved performance in the job he or she was hired to do—requires an atmosphere of open and honest communications throughout the entire organization. This means that open and honest employee relations must be the norm, requiring, in turn, a precondition of mutual respect for the dignity of all individuals.

An Open and Honest Atmosphere
Quality improvement cannot happen without an atmosphere of effective and honest communications, an atmosphere where mistakes are *not* made simply because people are afraid to ask. Nor is it ever likely to be attained by unhappy employees being manipulated by uninformed supervisors more concerned with office politics than the quality of work. For, in fact, quality improvement is not as much about standards as it is about winning the hearts and minds of all the people.

Every company has an existing communications system—some formal and rigidly controlled, others informal and uncontrolled. While too much emphasis at either of these extremes might cause problems for a company, a more important consideration is whether the communications are open and honest or restrained and manipulative.

Only an open and honest atmosphere has the potential to prevent or overcome serious credibility gaps between the company and its employees. This kind of honest relations also has the power to release the energies needed to *overcome and change the status quo,* primarily by driving *fear* out of the workplace. When employees are free of fear in their daily work environment, they are also free to become highly creative, interested, useful, and productive. They may even begin to take pleasure in their work. Can you imagine what a difference that would make in a company's pursuit of its business objectives?

Some years back, a company that produces high-grade cellulose introduced a quality improvement program at its largest and most modern mill. Part of the program involved quality improvement meetings with groups of pulp mill operators, who were unionized and historically unfriendly to management. To achieve some measure of credibility for these meetings, management decided to share and discuss current, intimate business facts with the employees. This became a milestone event because it addressed the biggest issue dividing management and labor at this mill.

Once the relationship was changed in this way, it was amazing how these people really opened up. Their knowledge of the work process and its most intimate problems was universal. Their up-front contributions to many challenging quality improvement opportunities were impressive and almost immediately successful. It was clear that these people, once moved from their traditional defensive position, were willing and able to contribute significantly to the start of quality improvement as an integrated process.

One measure of the quality of communications in a company is what happens when the existence of a major problem becomes known for the first time. Is it, as often happens, simply attributed to a breakdown in communications? More often than not, the real problem is a lack of adequate performance, lost in a quagmire of excessive communications, usually accompanied by some finger pointing.

This obstructive situation is common in many industrial areas. Its symptoms are embodied in everyone charging, or being driven, straight ahead, and then when something goes radically wrong, all in unison proclaim, ''It didn't happen here,'' ''I'm not responsible,'' or ''I tried to warn you.'' Is this the atmosphere in your company? If it is, quality starts here.

Vertical and Horizontal Communication

For communication to be effective, once its openness has been established, it must be reciprocal. That is, there is a sender, a receiver, and feedback to the sender to make sure the receiver truly understood the original message. Also, to be effective from an overall company point of view, communications must take place both horizontally and vertically.

Vertical communications usually means there is a network in place to push communications downward; but, in the spirit of quality improvement, there must also be a guarantee of an open, honest, and responsive formal system for the upward flow of communications. The horizontal communications needed are those that take place between peers, especially interfunctional peers.

Increased horizontal communication can help employees to understand their jobs better, by helping them see how their work fits in with the broader operations of the company. In fact, it would be helpful to the quality improvement program if each and every employee knew the answers to the following simple questions: What is my job? Where do I fit in the total company organization? Whom do I receive my work from? What do they do? Why do they do it? How do their failures affect me? Who receives the output from my work effort? What do they do? Why do they do it? How do my failures affect them?

There is no reason in the world why all employees shouldn't be free to think directly about the common good of the company, simply by being completely aware of where and how they fit into the overall picture.

Before embarking on a formal quality improvement program, a company can hardly afford *not* to have opened up these positive channels of communications, especially to give all employees the opportunity and encouragement to use the upward channel. For this specific purpose, and to help employees develop their communications skills, many employee communications programs are available in the marketplace.

It is critical to quality program success that the active participation of all employees be an important, up-front company consideration. Employees represent a reservoir of the most intimate knowledge about how the business really works. Management cannot afford to be without their inputs if there is to be any hope for true success. Don't leave communications to chance. Understand its intrinsic value to the achievement of quality improvement, and build its effective use throughout the company, right from the start.[1]

It takes two to speak the truth—one to speak, and another to hear.

Henry David Thoreau

Quality Education

Every company has a basic need to educate and train its employees. For some companies it is a major effort, for others it is not. But when a quality improvement program is involved, those responsible for education and training must significantly escalate their efforts.

Whether quality improvement for a company is a new system or a newly renovated old system, it is essential that all participants—that is, all employees—have knowledge of its principles, its value, its objectives, its tools and techniques, and the company's plan for implementation. This means educating them *why* quality improvement is being done and training them *how* it is to be done. The starting quality education effort should be designed to bring all employees through whatever state of confusion may initially exist, like leading them through a maze, to clearly see and understand the benefits to both themselves and the company (see Figure 6–4).

The experience of the eighties dictates being prepared to educate and train over and over again, as an ongoing, permanent part of the quality improvement process. It will of necessity become a major investment, but it will have an excellent return if entered into with the right attitude and a sense of its true worth. When years of neglect have, in effect, opened the doors for quality improvement to commence, a company cannot undo this state of being with a mediocre education and training effort. Employees, like children in a family, will know the true worth of the situation by the *actions* of management.

FIGURE 6–4
Quality Education

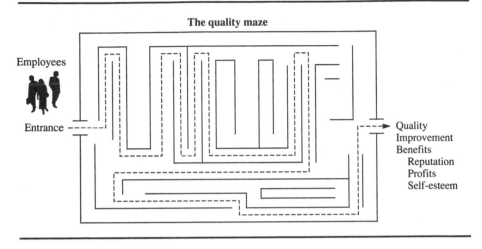

Evolution of Education Needs
In a sound education effort, each individual will learn to relate quality improvement to his or her own job responsibilities. Education is not for its own sake. It must enable movement toward quality program milestones. Training needs, on the other hand, evolve as the quality process takes hold.

Normally, a company will begin with the education of all levels of management, followed by the involvement of all employees in preparation for program start. Beyond this, the education and training program will grow as required throughout its full implementation. Some education and training needs will unfold as logical ingredients of the program as it moves ahead naturally. Other needs will only be required as the program, in fact, unfolds. Overall, there will be general quality improvement system education, special educational or training courses for different levels of participation, and specific training for quality improvement tools and techniques as their use evolves.

Continuous improvement is the rule with quality education as it is with the quality process itself. In the beginning, the training of many people is less important than training the right people—those who will serve as leaders, internal trainers, or coaches for the work groups that will be initially involved. The paramount goal of this initial effort, and all succeeding education efforts, is to get managers and employees to buy in to quality improvement by agreeing to take ownership of personal responsibility, innovation, and change.

Buying In to Quality Improvement

Everyone needs a certain level of understanding to buy in to the idea of quality improvement. Quality improvement is a new way of managing, not just another program; and it is long-term, not short-term. It has to be *believed* to work. If there is not true belief and personal commitment, it will not develop into a new way of industrial life.

Experience tells us that after the top executives are sold, the easiest people to convince are the working-level personnel, who really want to believe in the company and its programs. The toughest customers, and the most crucial to success, are the middle managers. Therefore, they need to be treated with tender loving care in an intense education and sales campaign.

In recent years, middle management has become a threatened species in many areas of industry. Often they are challenged to make things work, neglected when the big decisions are being made, overlooked when recognition is being handed out, and set up as scapegoats when things go wrong. The word is out that middle managers are expendable. Selling quality improvement in this kind of environment is a tough proposition. To accomplish it, therefore, a special effort must be made to win over each individual middle manager. What's really needed can be developed from the following:

1. Get them to see how the program benefits them personally. That is, get them to visualize how the program can help the company grow and prosper, and more specifically, how it can help them achieve their personal growth goals within the company. In other words, instill in them the idea, ''Instead of fighting it, make it work for you, personally.''

2. Get them to understand the business risks associated with inadequate quality performance. Show them how certain risks, internal to their function and interacting with other functions, have the potential to seriously affect their personal and their organization's business objectives.

3. Get them to understand the value of *quality work habits* and how specific quality tools can help their organization to perform better.

4. Get them to listen, over and over again, to the benefits of the program for themselves and the company.

There are many living proofs of the value in this approach. In a previous example (chapter 2), the material control manager who renamed his group ''the quality boosters'' is a middle manager who took advantage of the quality improvement program for the benefit of himself and the company. A young marketing director decided to become the quality leader for his company. Several years later, he became its president. In another case, a company president did so well in personally directing an outstanding recovery from major quality problems that he got to keep his job, and his quality improvement success story became a popular presentation at major quality conferences.

Getting a good start with the quality education of middle managers will ease the task of educating and training their personnel later on. It also has the potential to influence the development of much needed interfunctional teamwork.

Goals of Quality Education
Through education and training, participants in the quality improvement program should learn:

- The means for self-monitoring and self-correction that will encourage and help them to individually achieve continuous performance improvement.
- The personal satisfaction of applying new management concepts and techniques to accomplish their work responsibilities.

On the other hand, the following common mistakes need to be carefully avoided in the quality education program:

- Scheduling mass training before the support systems for the improvement program have been set up.
- Overemphasizing technical tools at the expense of leadership and participation issues.
- Getting involved with specific tools before the actual needs are determined.

To the quality professionals, quality improvement is a continuous business undertaking, not a onetime plateau of business performance to be reached. In this light, quality education is the way to prepare for and remain on the path of continuous improvement. To become educated means to develop mentally and morally, to become conditioned to believe or act in a certain way. That's exactly what's intended with quality system education—to become conditioned to believe in quality and to act in a disciplined manner to achieve it.

To succeed in quality improvement a company must make a major investment in quality education, easing off only when quality becomes part of the woodwork of all company performance—that is, when meeting quality requirements gets to be just like meeting the budget.

> *Enlighten the people generally, and tyranny and oppressions of body and mind will vanish like evil spirits at the dawn of day.*
>
> Thomas Jefferson

Recognition

Assume for the moment that in an atmosphere of open and honest communications, a company has taught and implemented a quality improvement process.

FIGURE 6–5
Heart of Quality Program

What's to keep this new system from falling into the same old, lackadaisical pattern of less-than-perfect attention and acceptance as we've seen so often happen with other management-supported, people-program innovations? The answer is *recognition*—the heart of quality improvement (see Fig 6–5).

Recognition that is honest, deserving, and sincere is so basic to good management that it would seem almost unnecessary to mention. It provides management with a tool to truly integrate people into the quality improvement system. Once quality measurements are in place and specific improvements are verified, formal recognition of individuals and groups—in a manner that they can appreciate and their associates can understand—is one of the best methods for sustaining personal interest and individual effort for continued quality progress.

Spontaneous recognition from supervisors and managers to employees is the most effective and inexpensive type available, especially if done in front of as many of the employee's peers as possible. Many quality surveys have pointed out that a primary desire of most employees is to be recognized by their boss for doing a good job. Failure to take advantage of this always available management tactic is a business blunder of the first order.

There are many types of recognition techniques available for company use. Examples include a picture and story in the company newsletter, lunch with the boss on a personal basis, formal special quality awards, periodic group dinners for meeting group quality goals, and anything else imaginable. Think about it as *celebrating quality progress.*

The personality and style of the company should strongly influence its formal program of recognition. There is no limit to its ultimate value. In all cases, the awards should never be trivial, nor should they be strictly monetary; and there must be absolutely no bias in any nominations and selections. Always remember that awards are intended to show respect for people and the important contributions they make. In a very significant way, however, formal recognition also helps to fulfill each person's human need for affirmation of self-worth.

The Improvement Process

So much has been written and said in recent years, under many different names, about the continuous improvement process, it is no wonder many business managers are confused and find it difficult to grasp. But it doesn't have to be complex.

A quality improvement process, under any name, involves just three basic, easily understood ingredients—measurements, analysis, and corrective action—applied toward increasing the achievement of quality requirements or standards. That's it, a simple, "new" supervisory tool to control and improve any work experience—even though its origin goes back over 50 years to the days of Dr. Walter Shewhart and the other pioneers of quality control for mass production. Each supervisor or frontline manager needs to learn this process and integrate it into his or her thinking. It is the blocking and tackling of quality improvement, and you will find it inherent to all available programs on the market.

Figure 6–6 typifies the basic improvement process. It starts with measurements of today's performance being collected and summarized into weekly reports for analysis and problem identification. The costliest problems are then investigated and analyzed to determine root causes and to ascertain and accomplish practical corrective actions, which will result in progressive performance improvement.

To fully understand the quality improvement process, let's examine each core ingredient, not in the sense of detailed planning for new program introduction, but in a more fundamental way. The following descriptions will illustrate the inherent logic and deep business design of each ingredient—central tasks that should become as ingrained in company operations as receiving a paycheck.

Measurement
For ease of description and understanding, *measurement* will be broken down into sampling, checking, and recording, the three elements that make up this starting point for the process.

Sampling.   This involves reaching into the entire gamut of company operations to see how each one is doing. More specifically, it means selecting a portion of all completed work for examination of the performance it represents. In many areas of company operations, performance information already exists but is not necessarily utilized for continuous quality improvement. In those areas where performance information is not readily available, management will have to plan

FIGURE 6–6
Quality Improvement Process

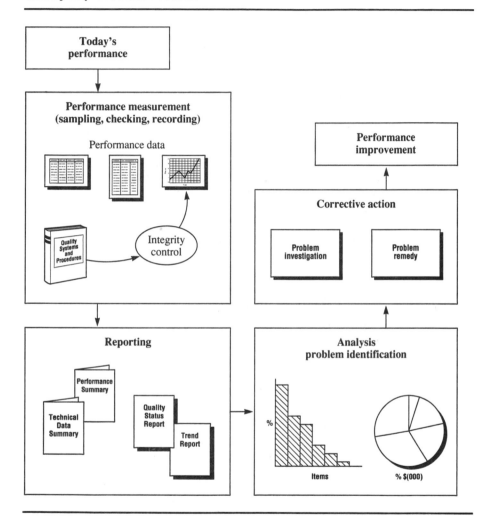

for and acquire it as a permanent part of the improvement process. Measurements of performance, like measurements of expenses, are forever.

The idea that people don't like to be measured is hogwash. Generally speaking, people believe in fair measurements. In fact most people, professional people included, need and desire the affirmation of their self-worth that normally comes from an honest evaluation of their performance. This particularly applies to good performers, who would indeed be penalized—or at least somewhat demotivated—without some ongoing confirmation of their satisfactory accomplishments.

On management's side, without periodic sampling or the use of data already available, supervisors and managers are unable to identify any but the most obvious performance problems. Nor are they able to recognize and reward outstanding performance, a genuine quality improvement asset. This thesis, of course, assumes that supervisors and managers know how to use performance measurements constructively.

Unfortunately for business in general, there seems always to be some percentage of poor performers, either by personal choice or by way of an undiscovered lack of capability. These performers welcome the opportunity to remain out of the spotlight. Probably well aware that they are underproducing, they don't wish to be discovered. They prefer the status quo. But this is anathema to quality improvement and one more reason why measuring performance is so important. It is not only wrong to protect underperformers, it is demoralizing to the good performers who are almost always aware when it is happening.

There is no set approach to the planning for this activity. It is ,however, the first major step supervisors take in the quality improvement process. Samples of completed work are normally taken at points within the operation that allow for evaluation of work process inputs, internal performance, and output. Selection of these points of quality measurement is correlated to:

1. *Customer satisfaction.* This is normally the result of the output of each interactive work process or each employee's individual work. This is the area that best relates to what the customers are most concerned about in their experience of quality.

Measurement of this area is most likely to find existing useful data that is not necessarily being utilized for improvement purposes. Examples of such missed opportunities include internal waste and rework, planning changes, billing errors, supplier rejects, late deliveries, accounting errors, and maintenance failures.

2. *Internal performance.* Measurement here should be based on what key measures determine how well and how consistently workers perform their tasks, or what characteristics of their work have the most impact on higher costs and customer complaints. If the area under consideration were a clerical or document-processing operation, the entire effort might simply be to focus on worker errors. In other words, look for a feedback measure of errors as delivered to internal and external customers, and supplement this with a continuous sampling of work in process. Use both items in combination to monitor and improve individual and group performance.

3. *Input quality.* Base the sampling here on what measures will advance the reduction or elimination of undesirable and costly characteristics in the materials or work in process supplied as input for the operation. Of course, this means first determining and clearly identifying the quality problems that exist in these inputs. All too often, inadequate quality results and the excess costs they generate are passed on from operation to operation. They become part of the accepted cost of doing business, simply because there is no formal program in place to constantly challenge their existence.

From a functional or technical requirements point of view, a broader perspective can be taken in developing the parameters for sampling. For example, consider the following illustrations:

- Comparing actual product or product-line sales to strategic sales forecasts can establish a track record for the always desired improvement of sales forecasting.

- Measuring variation in the cost of customer inquiries, complaints, and problems will shed light on the efficiency and effectiveness of the customer relations or service function and its ability to achieve internal corrective actions.

- Sampling credit memos can provide a key measure of the performance of a distribution center.

- Examining design changes and major unplanned technical support costs to early production can provide an important measure of new product or service development performance.

- Comparing actual production capabilities—involving people, equipment, tools, and processes—to specified requirements for 100 percent quality performance will serve as a measure of production planning results.

- Measuring production cost variances due entirely to supplier-caused problems, in conjunction with actual purchasing costs, is a better indicator of purchasing performance than the purchase costs alone.

Exactly where to sample or measure quality performance is limited only by the supervisor's detailed knowledge and imagination as he or she examines the opportunities truly available for personal and group performance improvement. The supervisor, however, will not be left alone in these deliberations. Specific guidance should come from the companywide quality program planning efforts.

Checking.   This is the act of measuring the sample against required work standards—the act of determining, in each case, whether or not the established quality performance standards have been achieved. Some measurements already exist as a normal part of company operations (e.g., production yields); for others, the checking can be accomplished by any qualified person, sometimes requiring the technical assistance of a computer or a piece of specialized equipment. Checking can be rudimentary, like examining a completed financial transaction for accuracy and adherence to the rules, or it can be judgmental, like evaluating an underwriting decision or a marketplace assessment. But in all cases, it must be performed by employees whose qualifications for the examination are beyond question.

The checking portion of the quality improvement process requires an authorized measurement plan and the availability of qualified, unbiased personnel. The most important criterion for implementation is that the checking responsibility become an integral part of the operation being measured, and not done by an independent, outside agency. This means that it must be accomplished by the same qualified people who are doing the work or by their supervisor. The preference is integrated peer evaluation, with the supervisor serving as backup.

Whether applied to individual results or at the end of an interactive work process, checking has to become an integral part of everyday work assignments to ensure companywide *continuous* improvement. For supervision, this means ownership of the process, as opposed to just keeping things moving. If this concept seems too big an effort, too big a risk, or too unreasonable a demand, forget quality improvement. This is the raw material for the alchemy of today's business prosperity.

When the checking takes place at the end of a work process involving people and machinery, no one person is alone responsible for the end result—but all involved people should be keenly aware of and knowledgeable about the technical quality standards for the process output. Being periodically assigned to assess how well these results are being achieved can only serve to sharpen the overall knowledge and interest of all the participants.

In checking that involves judgment, the most senior members of the team and the supervisor will have to carry the burden. In all cases, the checking portion of the quality improvement process must be planned, organized, assigned, and scheduled. And as supervisors become finessed in performing this important task, they should develop and more fully utilize the talents of all group members.

The management advantage of including checking as an integral and normal part of all work processes is that nobody can shirk their basic responsibility for quality performance without it being noticed. Employees are not only constantly aware that their output will be evaluated, they must themselves contribute to the evaluation process.

(The next chapter, "Personal Guidelines for the Journey," will describe the logical transition of the sampling and checking effort into self-directed teams. This discussion has served to lay a workable foundation and to present the business reasons for these fundamental tasks.)

Recording. This formal documentation of the results of checking—the quality "facts"—will become the prime input for performance evaluation and improvement. Collectively, these facts identify the major types and quantities of errors or nonconformances that are occurring. This is the exact input needed to pursue problem identification, cause determination, and corrective action. To facilitate this action, the data must be recorded in a form suitable for the purpose. This simply means that a form be designed for each different situation.

Basically, the form merely needs to allow the recording of data about each sample and about the specific results. Typical of the initial data required for each sample is the identification of the sample; the date and time; the type, variation, or batch number of output represented; and the person who did the checking.

Once the sample is identified, the form needs to allow for recording the occurrence of satisfactory or unsatisfactory results, based on current process standards and experience. This section of the recording format is dynamic; that is, the initial list of expected problem categories may not be applicable later as major causes of problems are eliminated or drastically reduced. Thus, minor problems originally included under "miscellaneous" may later have to be re-identified as problems that require evaluation and action.

All other errors, complaints, and nonconformances discovered within the responsible unit—or those discovered downstream for which the unit is responsible—also need to be documented for use in the analysis of results. If all available performance data are not utilized in the analysis of performance, the picture will not be complete.

In a particular lighting products company some years ago, the manufacturing operation had its own inspection function to weed out defects before the quality inspector discovered them at the end of the production line. During the implementation of a quality measurement system, manufacturing supervisors thought it was unfair to count the defects discovered and corrected or scrapped by their own people. They saw their quality responsibility as starting at the *end of the production line.*

In this case, the manufacturing organization completely failed to get the point that quality improvement is aimed at eliminating the cost of *all defects,* not just those that escape their area of activity. This kind of parochial thinking is very likely to be repeated in any organization that is new to quality improvement.

Measurement Benefit. In an overall sense, utilizing the continuous improvement process for either a manufacturing or service business means that in each area of company activity, the results of work performed is sampled and checked to determine its conformance to the standard or to indicate an opportunity for improvement. It further means that an important part of each supervisor's responsibility is to measure and validate quality performance—just like compiling time and expenses against a budget—and to initiate appropriate corrective action in a continuous effort to improve the quality of all results.

An unintended off-grade result occurs periodically in some companies. For example, companies that employ a continuous process (e.g., chemical, food, or raw materials processing) with variable natural resource inputs face an unappealing business situation whenever the process output fails to meet planned target values. The only way it can be sold is to match it to a particular customer's current needs. This is called "finding a customer for what gets made."

While this exercise is a good one for salvage operations, it must never be allowed to become a routine event. The danger is that company sales groups will become so expert in this practice that they unwittingly remove the need for production supervisors to consistently achieve outputs that meet the original quality requirements—thus sowing the seeds for the opposite of quality progress.

Consider the basic role of the supervisor to acquire and utilize quality measurements for continuous performance improvement. What more important business responsibility could be established at this crucial level of company management? Or what better arrangements could possibly be made for supervision to encourage and empower individual employee contributions to company progress, and for bestowing appropriate employee recognition? What a great way, also, for supervisors to prepare for the coming of self-directed teams and to use *coaching* as a supervision tool. Can you imagine a coach working without data about performance? Without a measurement practice in place, all but the most obvious performance inadequacies won't even be discovered by the supervisor, and they will be paid for *over and over again.*

The potential results of the lack of quality measurement as a management tool can be seen in the following story from a large foundry operation. A study of scrap experience for this foundry showed a definite pattern of long-term variation. The recorded scrap rate seemed to be slowly changing, from a high of 9 percent to a low of 6 percent and then back again, every three to three and a half years.

While it could never be proven, it seemed that what was actually happening was a manipulation of the scrap rates. At the higher rates, management screamed for action because the cost was clearly hurting. This brought on attempts to eliminate poor performance habits that had slowly crept into the work processes. Scrap rates then started to go down. Much later, after management had removed pressure, the scrap rates began to slowly rise again.

The good news of this story is that the actual scrap rate for this foundry was ultimately reduced to 3 percent several years after management adopted and implemented formal quality measurement and improvement.

Fundamentally, the purpose of quality improvement is to improve performance; and the purpose of quality measurement is to identify the problems whose solutions embody this improvement. Measuring quality performance is different and more powerful than just measuring schedule and costs. Quality measures not only tell a company how well they are doing, but how well they can ultimately do. Therein lies the power and the opportunity. Just meeting schedule and cost goals can never accomplish that (see Figure 6–7).

FIGURE 6–7
The Power of Quality Measurements

	Cost and Schedule Measurements	Quality Measurements
What is measured	How well we performed against the budget and the schedule.	How well we performed against the required work standards.
What is the objective?	Are we still tracking to the plan, or does something need a quick fix?	Are customers being served, or is improvement needed?
Who is served?	Serves executive needs, with no obvious concern for employees or customers.	Serves customer needs; supervisors learn how to focus improvement.
What are the benefits?	Financial reporting and executive decision making.	Employee relations and customer satisfaction.
Best results possible?	Short-term continuation.	Long-term power.

In summary, the measurement function—sampling, checking, and recording—assesses actual performance as compared to the quality requirements established by the company. It does this by examining part of the input, value added, and output for each segment of work—direct and indirect, production and support. It identifies levels of performance and types of nonconformances. Its results identify real improvement opportunities, involving individuals and their support systems, interfunctional support systems, general business support systems, and the company's management system.

Quality measurement is an activity where a clear-cut level of investment must be determined and authorized. Like financial performance, quality performance must be measured. Quality improvement is not just a philosophy. It is a doable and important business undertaking. But it will not succeed if the supervisor, or self-directed team, is not provided with the necessary resources, such as man-hours, training, and applicable tools, to carry out the planned measurements. Nor will it succeed if the supervisor is too easily distracted from this vital responsibility for inappropriate reasons, like "too many administrative tasks" or "too much fire fighting."

With what measure ye mete, it shall be measured to you.

Mark 4:24

FIGURE 6–8
Common Data Analysis Tools

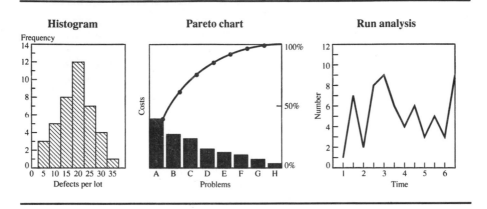

Within the accepted level of the agreed-upon effort for each functional area, collections of quality measurements can be assembled and reported as a trend—thus illuminating the current level of quality performance for the area and whether this performance is, in fact, getting better or worse. Also in each area, continued quality improvement will be advanced whenever new performance objectives are established and pursued.

This constant quest for improvement logically leads to the next step in the improvement process, which is to analyze the types of nonconformances found in each area to determine the most significant negative cost contributors to the quality performance being reported. The elimination of these major contributors is the most profitable avenue for improvement action—that is, the most profitable way to spend investigative and corrective action dollars. Essentially, it is the relentless pursuit of these nitty-gritty problems that will collectively make up the bulk of available improvement progress. Miracle onetime solutions to America's quality problems are long gone.

Analysis

Analysis is the application of certain techniques (see Figure 6–8) to the quality data to determine the most significant contributors to all failures to achieve 100 percent quality performance. Once the raw data from checking and all other sources have been recorded for the sampling period, they can be separated into two categories of performance: (1) data about performance of individual workers, and (2) data about performance that is the output of combinations of people, equipment, and supplies. Next, the data in each of these two categories can be reorganized for the following uses:

- To compile overall period performance results for comparison with recent past history as a measure of quality progress.

- To construct a summary distribution matrix of findings to facilitate selection of the next most significant problem, or *person* in the case of individual output measurements, for subsequent investigation and corrective action.

In essence, organize the data so it can "talk to you."

The chronology of supervisory actions is an important part of the management of improvement. So far, we've discussed the events of the improvement process as individual ingredients of progress. Now, let's look at their relationships. Since the discussion is essentially about a quality improvement process intended for the continuous and universal use of all supervisors, let's look at its practical utility as opposed to what some may view as just a lot of extra work or additional activities, with the implied connotation that it may or may not produce results.

By now the clear message should be that the continuous improvement process is a results-oriented strategy. It is strictly aimed at people and work processes. Its intent is to help employees grow in job performance and to quickly identify and eliminate the most significant work-process problems. It is long-term and persistent—not quick and dirty, or sporatic. The amount of investment required relates to current business realities in the world marketplace.

From a practical point of view, collecting performance sampling data on a weekly basis seems entirely reasonable. Of course, the amount of data a company needs to identify major problems is a lot less than that needed if it were applying precise statistical process controls. Common sense also suggests that monthly compilation of data for analysis and corrective action is reasonable in most situations. Any company that can't afford this amount of improvement effort on the part of all supervision is a company that can't afford progress.

Corrective Action

Corrective action is founded on the premise, "There are no economics of quality," which means:

1. For each failure, there is a root cause.
2. Causes are preventable.
3. Prevention is always cheaper.

In practice, corrective action is the application of investigative and problem-solving techniques (see Figure 6–9 for some examples) to each identified problem for the express purpose of:

1. Determining and identifying the underlying cause of the problem.
2. Taking the necessary remedial action to eliminate the identified root cause.
3. Verifying that the cause removal has indeed corrected the originally identified problem.

FIGURE 6–9
Common Investigative Techniques

Brainstorming

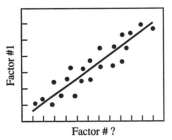

Work flow analysis (WFA)

Supplier

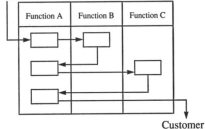

Customer

Correlation analysis

Cause and effect diagrams

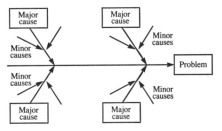

Input/output analysis

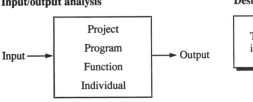

Design of experiments

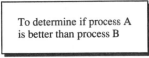
To determine if process A is better than process B

When the problems to be corrected are clearly caused by people not performing up to their potential or up to the demonstrated capability of the unit, the supervisor's role in people development is greatly enhanced. With the continuous results of sampling and analysis available, it shouldn't be too difficult to imagine how much easier and how much more effective the supervisor can be in fulfilling this important human relations responsibility, even more so when remedial action is indicated. The more that is known about each employee's performance, the more able the supervisor is to place them in the right jobs and then to supervise their continued personal development.

When the problems to be corrected involve the business system or technical aspects, all available investigative tools, techniques, and methodologies should be brought into play, with no holds barred. Sincere attempts to find the root causes of problems, and then to find or create the means to prevent them from happening again, have provided the substance for much of the technical quality progress that has been achieved over the past two decades.

Corrective action cannot be legislated; it must be worked at. A good example of what corrective action *is not* occurred at an industrial heating system company a few years ago. A new operations director had been hired to, among other things, solve their quality problems. For at least three years this company had been unconscionably tolerating a product final test rejection rate of between 20 and 25 percent and a warranty return rate of 7 percent. After six months of weekly corrective action meetings, there was no discernable change in results.

This dynamic leader's idea of corrective action was to demand answers from the foremen, engineers, and other involved personnel, without providing the resources for adequate investigation. Each week problem causes were *forcibly suggested* and corrective action was committed to—actions like work-process changes and engineering design changes. Most of the actions probably did some good, but in general, they did not solve major problems. Unfortunately, under these dynamic management conditions, which the company president strongly supported, there wasn't any real corrective action.

THE NEED FOR QUALITY SYSTEMS

The conscientious execution of the improvement process has always ignited, as it will continue to ignite, new developments in the techniques of quality control and improvement. If a solution to your particular problem does not exist, commitment to this process can motivate you to create a solution.

In administrative and service businesses, exposures to possible failure to conform to the standard are no different than they are in manufacturing operations. Failures that result in complaints, waste, or reprocessing are committed by the work-process developers, by the designers and fabricators of support tools and equipment, by those who determine process capabilities or limitations, by those who provide second-level inputs to direct support processes, and by those who provide the written instructions and training for the employees who perform the work.

Other failures that affect service quality results can be committed by maintenance personnel, stock clerks, billing clerks, buyers, accountants, and other general support personnel. Almost anyone in the entire organization is capable of inadvertently contributing to or causing less-then-achievable results—otherwise, it would be well to question their real business purpose or value.

Some types of performance failures that negatively affect work-process results will become obvious when causes are pursued as an integral part of the improvement process. These include inadequate training and, of course, outright failures to execute the planned work process. But other types of failure may not be so obvious, such as a marginal or barely achievable work process, marginal equipment, or in the worst case, marginal reception by the customer of the process output. These kinds of failure demand a formal system to prevent them from becoming lost or buried in the accepted risks and costs of the business.

Genuine efforts to resolve the most challenging and overlooked or, in the worst case, tolerated problems can prove to be the most interesting and rewarding part of the improvement process. Finding the root cause of previously unsolved company problems is a pioneering effort. It adds knowledge where it did not exist before.

An effective, steady quality improvement process not only provides the means for such significant benefits, it ultimately leads to the routine identification of problems *before* they can become serious. On the other hand, a company without a continuous improvement process can, at the very best, only hope for the status quo, today's perennial nemesis.

In review, the continuous quality improvement process is designed to measure and expose, in all areas of company business, undesirable conditions that cause excess costs or lost revenues. Such conditions might otherwise be hidden from management because they are buried somewhere within the woodwork of the current management system (see Figure 6–10).

Figure 6–10 presents Juran's Quality Trilogy, a representation of the improvement opportunity available in almost any human endeavor. The cost of poor quality continues unabated at an unacceptable level *until* formal quality improvement is implemented; then there is a succession of improved levels achieved in a continuous march toward 100 percent performance.

An effective improvement process has the substance to become a practical tool for efficient cost trade-offs and permanent reductions in the standard operating cost of a company. At the same time, it can dramatically improve the company's productivity and quality reputation. That's why it is so important that all supervision be energetically involved.

FIGURE 6–10
Juran's Quality Trilogy

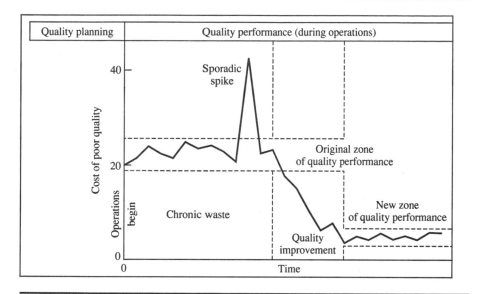

Source: A. Blanton Godfrey, "Part II, Strategic Quality Management," *Quality Progress,* April 1990, pp. 27–29. Adapted by permission.

SUMMARY

As stated earlier, implementing only the improvement process or structured part of the improvement system is not enough. In fact, it will not work alone. Genuine success depends on the wholesomeness of the business atmosphere within which the improvement process is expected to operate—that is, the openness, mutual respect, friendly attitudes, and cooperation that each employee can expect to experience daily. This clearly entails open and honest communications, sequential education, and formal recognition of exceptional efforts. In essence, this is the nourishment necessary for companywide quality improvement to continue bearing its fruit.

Underlying this broad concept is the fundamental idea that the purpose of quality improvement is to "improve quality . . . period." In this sense, quality improvement is directly and solely aimed at the prevention of inadequate quality performance—as discovered through quality measurement, eliminated through corrective action, and prevented from reoccurrence through the incorporation of effective quality disciplines.

Prevention is probably the most important but, at the same time, the most misunderstood word in the entire concept of quality improvement. It is a lot easier said than done, representing a relentless challenge to grow. It is always a tough proposition because it demands basic changes in the way work is performed and managed. That is, it challenges you to continuously develop better work habits—quality work habits—utilizing the tools of total quality management and remaining focused on customer satisfaction. There is no better way for an organization to grow in overall performance. And there is no easier way to beat the competition.

Each and every time work is to be authorized, performed, or approved, there is a built-in opportunity to prevent a problem by simply assessing what, if anything, is *likely to go wrong.* Can you imagine the benefits to a company if just once every week all employees, especially those in management, would sincerely ask themselves: "How many times have *I* missed the opportunity to prevent a problem?"

The ultimate goal of the central quality system is building quality improvement into the thinking and actions of every employee. In its broadest sense it can be viewed as going through a series of phases:

- Phase 1 occurs when people are uneducated and unknowledgeable about the personal and business value of a companywide quality improvement system—that is, *people are in the dark.*

- Phase 2 occurs when people are introduced to the concepts of quality improvement and given the opportunity to evaluate it for themselves— that is, *people are aware.*

- Phase 3 occurs when people have decided to buy in to the program and engage themselves to act with quality clearly in mind—that is, *people are committed.*

- Phase 4 occurs when doing a quality job and seeking continuous quality improvement become part of the woodwork of company operations—that is, *people are integrated* into the quality system, and *quality is integrated* into the management system.

This fundamental concept of quality improvement, or *managing by quality,* by its very nature indicates why quality improvement is primarily viewed as a people program. It is aimed at people. It involves people. And its rewards are due to people responding in a positive way. It is a potential gold mine of people power. And it is loaded with people benefits. It fosters respect for associates on every level. It encourages honesty in all dealings involving the company. It prevents finger pointing by allowing people freedom to make mistakes while trying creatively to improve. Instead of discouraging change, it anticipates and welcomes constructive change. It is a people program par excellence.

A customized companywide quality improvement program can be developed to meet the unique organizational needs of any specific company. But this unique program must then belong totally to the company, in the same way that a newly developed product or process belongs to the company. It must be accepted and managed, as is a newly imposed legal procedure, until it ultimately becomes integrated into the woodwork of the operations. If this key and costly point, the need for management ownership, is not fully appreciated up front, it may be better not to start.

Many program failures have been a direct result of key managers not accepting the quality improvement program as their own, at best cheering it on but in no way leading it. These managers somehow expect performance improvement to be generated up and down the organization from somewhere in between, conveniently forgetting that they are the ones paid to make things happen. This program will never compensate for management deficiencies; but in a constructive sense, it will help to identify and eliminate them. And it has an excellent potential for building better managers.

Companies that are not yet open to the business value of quality improvement will soon find themselves left behind in the marketplace, if that has not already happened. On the other hand, those companies that are interested, and that may still be struggling with basic concepts, will find exactly what they need in the next section—guidelines for their own unique journey.

CHAPTER 7

PERSONAL GUIDELINES FOR THE JOURNEY[1]

The philosophy of total quality management (TQM), as an overall promotion, was introduced and briefly described in Chapter 5. We then examined the central idea that makes this ultimate quality system work, focusing on the underlying principles and strategic practices involved. Now we need to understand those core concepts of TQM in an instructional way to prepare the *people* to make TQM work. Only with the full knowledge and acceptance of these guidelines can you professionally prepare for and hope to realize the full potential of TQM.

This is it! Now that you've seen the big picture, this is the *prescription* you need to tie together all that has been previously presented, to truly meet the challenge of TQM, and to clearly envision the required investments in people and time. These bedrock disciplines provide all you need to know for improving personal effectiveness and performance, and for including and aligning all individual efforts throughout an organization, regardless of its size.

In essence, the incremental integration of these guidelines into daily work habits is a lengthy process, but it is the best and perhaps only way to truly build the company infrastructure needed to support the continuous improvement process. It is also a way to leverage individual effort, extending its effect and importance throughout an organization and beyond. And this can be done in any business environment, even those with serious constraints on organizational resources and time.

Total quality management is not a destination, but a journey along the way of improvement, a journey routinely laced with outstanding personal performance and breakthrough results. These guidelines will show exactly how to get started and remain on this journey. They will shed additional light on the benefits of continuous improvement, but they will also highlight the challenges of and responsibilities for leading the improvement effort in an organization.

Those who have blazed the trail of continuous quality improvement have left us a legacy of lessons learned. Many had false starts or traveled down dead-end roads and had to start over. If there is one consistent lesson from these pioneers, it is that there is no universal strategy for success. The road to continuous improvement is and must be appropriately tailored and personal. A general behavior pattern and set of actions, however, characterize most successful efforts. For those who choose to follow, that *behavior* and those *actions* are presented here as a reliable road map for the TQM journey.

The way to quality fulfillment is not easy. It is interlaced with many difficult and demanding management conversions, true tests of management's commitment, courage, and perseverance. It will normally take years to reach maturity in TQM, years of learning, working differently, and growing in ability and achievement. It will also, most certainly, be personally rewarding, as illustrated by the spontaneous statement of an old line supervisor caught up in the fervor of full-time TQM: "Never in my life have I had so much fun working so hard and learning so much." But make no mistake about it, choosing this path is not easy. It is an act of *tough love* by its leaders to strengthen or save a business.

DEMONSTRATE LEADERSHIP

Total quality management depends on people more than anything else; and people either lead or they are led, they are not managed. *To manage quality, you must lead people.* Effective TQM depends on effective leadership. When leaders take the initiative, provide the example, and show the way, employees can be led and peers can be inspired. Superiors may even decide to follow. Effective TQM leadership does not depend on position in the organization but rather on the communication of enthusiasm and visible commitment to the process of continuous improvement.

The following actions can help achieve this behavior pattern:

1. *Take the initiative.* Demonstrate the behavior expected of employees, after taking the time necessary to learn and develop some expertise in that behavior. Demonstrating TQM before mandating it shows that you are serious about its implementation and believe in its potential. For those processes the leader is directly involved in, he or she should visibly and consistently apply the improvement philosophy and appropriate practices. Thus the leader can gain expertise and demonstrate sincerity, while preparing the way for sharing the lessons learned and assisting subordinates in their implementation.

2. *Demonstrate commitment.* Leading the way means demonstrating commitment to the TQM philosophy, principles, and practices on a daily basis. Demonstration means espousing the beliefs you wish to be established in others and then *living those beliefs* by exhibiting the behavior that logically arises from them. Show commitment by personally participating in TQM activities; by willingly leading employees and *enabling* them to improve their processes; by establishing clear, achievable, agreed-upon improvement goals; and by exhibiting a forthright passion for improvement.

3. *Create more leaders.* Leadership is not monopolistic. Continuous improvement needs leaders at all levels and in all parts of the company organization. Generate leaders among employees by giving them increased responsibility with commensurate authority to improve their processes and by providing the training and resources needed to carry out those improvements. TQM leaders can also be generated among peers and superiors when continuous improvement successes are demonstrated and awareness is transformed into genuine interest. The more leaders are created, the more successful TQM will be throughout the entire company organization.

4. *Guide the efforts of others.* A key principle of continuous improvement is that individuals and groups learn from their mistakes, but only when they are able to compare *actual* behavior and results with *expected* behavior and results. Mistakes must be forgiven if people are to be free to learn. TQM is about learning—with no place for judgments that serve only to inhibit the learning process and impede the way of improvement. Every improvement payoff is the culmination of an individual's or a group's learning and contributions, encouraged by the leader's coaching and recognition.

5. *Remove roadblocks and barriers.* Leaders must identify and remove the roadblocks and barriers that impede continuous improvement efforts. Removing these impediments will allow people to move ahead, to strengthen their abilities, and to increase their will to improve. Encourage employees to identify those barriers that are preventing them from reaching their personal improvement goals. Barriers may be physical or psychological, and they exist between individuals, groups, or elements of the management system. In all cases, eliminate identified barriers or, at the very least, minimize them to the extent possible.

BUILD AWARENESS

Building awareness—the understanding of what TQM is and why it is important to the organization—is an important first step in the implementation of TQM. Every person in the organization must become aware of the need to improve, of the *promise* offered by TQM, and of the various methodologies and tools available to support the effort.

Here's how to use awareness as the key to open the door of TQM's potential:

1. *Generate personal awareness.* Personal awareness is essential to the implementation of TQM. It applies to every person on the journey. It means understanding the philosophy of continuous improvement; learning about process improvement methodologies, skills, and techniques; sharing this knowledge with superiors, peers, and employees; and using it to guide your own personal improvement effort.

2. *Read appropriate literature.* A wide body of literature addresses the theories and practices that support TQM's practical efforts; this book is devoted to that objective. Using this book as the foundation, you can sort out and evaluate prospective programs and then design and guide a TQM effort that best meets the specific needs of your organization.

3. *Attend TQM workshops and conferences.* Meetings, seminars, and classes offered by recognized leaders in TQM can be instrumental in building awareness. No two approaches are exactly alike, but all courses generally offer common lessons in developing core skills. And the unique experiences of the course instructors and other attendees will provide additional benefits.

4. *Help the top manager become more aware.* Gaining the support of the company's upper management will play a major role in the ultimate success or failure of the TQM effort. The top manager's behavior will either enhance TQM progress or unacceptably restrict it. Therefore, encouraging his or her personal awareness and participation in the effort will greatly improve its chances for success. It will also help with the upward—and downward—movement of personal commitment to TQM in the total organization.

5. *Discuss TQM with peers.* Horizontal communication among peers is as important to the success of TQM as is vertical communication between superior and employees. Discussing TQM with peers and spreading enthusiasm for its potential benefits will encourage peers to undertake their own efforts. This, in turn, will open the door to the sharing of common lessons and the addressing of interfunctional problems and issues that frequently deter progress.

6. *Help employees become more aware.* The help and support of employees is an essential ingredient for any TQM effort, but the opportunity and conditions to *enable* that support must be present. Encourage employee awareness by providing education and training classes and actively participating in the improvement process. And your enthusiasm can be infectious.

7. *Share the concept with union leadership.* Unions are powerful elements in an organization. They are attuned to attitudes and concerns of their membership and have significant influence over their members' reactions to an organization's initiatives. Union leaders should be educated in the objectives of TQM, and they should be involved in setting goals and supporting joint management/union improvement activities. Union involvement will help reduce the fear of—or resistance to—TQM, and it will increase the chances for full and uncompromised participation by employees and peers. When customers and employees are the most important parts of the TQM effort, union and management will share the same goals.

8. *Inform customers and suppliers.* A fundamental principle of TQM is to build close relationships with customers and suppliers, maintaining frequent contact with them. This can start with the company communicating to customers and suppliers its plans to embark on a TQM journey, with an explanation of why this is happening and how it will affect them. If the customers and suppliers are not familiar with TQM concepts and practices, you may offer or suggest educational materials for them to use as resources. It is also important to solicit their ideas on how to work more closely and productively together.

OPEN AND MAINTAIN LINES OF COMMUNICATION

Honest, open communication is the most important factor in successfully creating a healthy environment for the implementation of TQM. As work progresses in building awareness throughout the organization, clear lines of communication must be either confirmed or opened up both horizontally and vertically. Doing this may take time, but it will lead to trust and mutual respect among all company personnel—empowering them to work through problems, overcome barriers, and provide encouragement and support for each other.

Create a productive communications atmosphere through the use of these two steps:

1. *Open up all channels of communication.* Communication requires both a sender (talker) and a receiver (listener). Leaders must learn to do a lot of listening. Good communication often involves *knowing what questions to ask, carefully listening to the answers, and then acting on the answers.* Progress requires that horizontal and vertical communications be free and open throughout the organization—that is, they must be as unrestricted as possible. Constrained communications will quickly eliminate any atmosphere of trust that has developed. It is important, then, to open up new channels of communication as they are needed, and to keep all channels open.

2. *Keep everyone informed.* Individuals become dissatisfied when kept in the dark about the organization's goals, their superior's objectives, or even what is expected of them personally. But if the leader continuously shares management information, goals, and objectives, never works from a hidden agenda, and establishes a policy of "no surprises," followers will feel more secure, and they will contribute freely and honestly to the implementation of TQM.

CREATE A CONSTANCY OF PURPOSE

Constancy of purpose establishes a common direction for all organizational elements, and it ensures that efforts at all levels contribute to the achievement of broad objectives relevant to the entire organization. Communicating the organization's goals and objectives throughout all functions is essential to the focusing of improvement efforts for the common benefit. The leader's behavior and attitudes must always reinforce this constancy of purpose.

To manifest this type of behavior:

1. *Examine the organization's mission.* An organization's mission is a formal statement of its overriding goals and objectives, without which there is no way for its members to be entirely clear about their assignment. This statement should relate the organization's understanding of its customers' needs, requirements, and expectations; it should convey a commitment to this sense of purpose; and it should portray a vision of the organization's future.

2. *Take a long-term view.* The vision of where the organization is going with its TQM effort should be based on the organization's values, and it should promote behavior that is consistent with these values. Any vision of continuous improvement must have at its heart the betterment of each individual with a stake in the organization, and this must be clearly communicated to all. Strategic planning, the means by which an organization's mission and vision are translated into operational goals and objectives, must include as one of its primary elements an overriding mandate to improve all organizational processes.

3. *Establish meaningful goals.* The strategic planning process yields both long-term goals and specific goals that are the short-term opportunities for the improvement effort. Perhaps the most important characteristic of all goals is that they be challenging as well as reasonable and achievable. The supporting detail plans, in turn, must be realistic, focusing on the methods for achieving the desired results and always grounded in the idea that the primary goal is *continuous improvement* in customer satisfaction.

4. *Effectively deploy policy throughout the organization.* The best goals and objectives throughout the organization will be meaningless if they are not coordinated and aligned with the organization's mission. Policy deployment provides the means by which broad organizational goals are iteratively translated into more specific goals and objectives for eventual improvement actions. Such deployment is accomplished by viewing the organization as a linkage of processes in which no individual or group operates in a vacuum. Goals are then developed and acted upon within the framework of this linkage.

5. *Treat goals and performance carefully.* As people attempt to reach a numeric goal, they have a choice of three methods:

a. Improve the system.

b. Distort the system—that is, get the demanded results at the expense of other results.

c. Distort the figures.

In TQM, people are expected to improve the system. However, if people are *judged* on the basis of the achievement of results, they will often distort the system or distort the figures. Therefore, leaders must always base performance reviews on how people are going about improving the system rather than on whether or not they are reaching numeric goals.

6. *Ensure that behavior and signals are consistent with goals.* Nothing can thwart a TQM effort more than a leader's overt behavior that signals to the organization's members a lack of sincerity about or commitment to the philosophy and principles of TQM. All new policies and initiatives must reflect the organization's mission and vision and be consistent with TQM principles and practices. Old policies and initiatives must be revised as well. Once a leader establishes credibility in TQM, all of his or her behavior must reinforce that dedication and commitment.

7. *Align overall improvement activity with organizational goals.* Individual and group improvement activities are the means by which organizational goals are realized. Therefore, aligning these improvement activities with the overall goals is crucial to a successful effort. A big step toward this is to organize process improvement teams and link them vertically. Next, align goals horizontally by using cross-functional teams. (Team organization and development is discussed later.)

FOCUS ON THE CUSTOMER

Every process in the organization has a customer; without a customer, a process has no purpose. The customer is the recipient of the process's products or services and is, therefore, the one who determines the quality requirements. It is only through focusing on the customer that an organization can truly optimize its processes, because it is only through the customer that goals and objectives for improvement can be effectively defined. This focus includes the organization's external customers, and its internal customers, members of the organization who depend on intra-organizational products or services for their own processes.

Here are the steps for putting the customer in proper focus:

1. *Link organizational purpose to customer satisfaction.* The customer defines the purpose of the organization and every process within it. Success means striving to become the best supplier of particular products and services in the minds of those customers. To achieve this success, the organization must align its overriding strategic vision with one of complete customer service and satisfaction; it must then apply this vision to each organizational process with respect to its internal customers as well.

Each process, within the context of the improvement effort, needs to be monitored constantly for progress. It is important that perceived improvements be equally perceptible to customers. Inquiring as to the suitability of planned improvements should be part of the continuous dialogue established with customers. Because the organization and its processes exist to serve the customer, improvements are of no benefit if they do not clearly benefit the customer.

2. *Identify external and internal customers.* Identifying customers is the first step in developing a customer focus. External customers are easy to identify; they are *outside* the organization but have formal relationships with it. Internal customers are another matter. All processes must be assessed to determine who *in the organization* receives process outputs and benefits from them, or should benefit from them. These are the internal customers, and they should be made aware that they are customers.

3. *Understand customer needs, expectations, and requirements.* Satisfying the customer means that the products and services generated by the processes meet their needs. To meet these needs, they must first be understood. Customers will have specific requirements that are peculiar to their own operations and concerns. They will expect a certain level of performance from the organization and its products. They may also have *implicit* needs that they do not normally articulate but that are equally important. As a supplier, the organization is responsible to ensure that all customer needs, requirements, and expectations are identified, and that they are mutually understood and agreed upon.

4. *Establish routine and meaningful dialogue with customers.* Continuous discussions of customers' needs and how well they are being met is crucial to effective customer service. The agreed-upon understanding must be continually updated in the context of a constantly changing environment, both the customer's and the organization's. The organization must also communicate its needs for feedback and information from its customers.

5. *Listen to the customer.* More important than merely talking to the customer is *listening* to the customer. Customers' true needs can only be discovered by listening and observing, in their own work areas if possible. To ensure adequate understanding of the customers' biases and preferences, the organization should listen *before* supplying its own preferences to the discussion. By listening to its customers, the organization will gain an improved understanding of its own performance.

6. *Involve the customer in planning and decision making.* Planning and decision making can be much more effective when customers are involved. This does not mean that the customers should control or manipulate the planning process; rather, they should communicate their needs directly into the organization's planning and strategic focus. Because they are the foundation of the organization's goals and objectives, customers can provide information that is directly beneficial to the planning process.

DEVELOP TEAMWORK

Teamwork is the engine that drives many improvement efforts. Creating teams allows the application of diverse skills and experience to problem solving and process improvement. Teams provide a basis of experience and history to the improvement effort, and they are the primary vehicles through which all individuals are enabled to participate in the effort. Not only must individuals cooperate within teams, the teams must cooperate together throughout the organization. An atmosphere of teamwork should permeate the organization, affecting not only formal team efforts but also each individual's interaction in the organization.

To develop teamwork in your TQM effort:

1. *Facilitate team development and activity.* Teams will not just develop of their own accord. Barriers will often have to be broken down between and inside organizations to enable team formation. Management approaches built on goal development that is independent of an overriding organizational vision and strategy create barriers, because they permit conflicting and counterproductive goals. It is important to ensure that teams develop goals and pursue improvements that reinforce one another, as well as the organization's constancy of purpose. Teamwork in TQM is not merely employee involvement, it is the *management of participation.*

Every team should be working continuously to improve its processes; otherwise, the concept of continuous improvement does not work. When this systematic approach to improvement is used, ongoing efforts may take on the appearance of a series of projects, which they often are. The ultimate goal, nevertheless, is to make this technique *the way* process maintenance and improvement is routinely accomplished throughout the organization.

2. *Create cross-functional teams for cross-functional purposes.* Many of the organization's problems will not be confined to one functional group. Cooperation among peers is used to solve these problems, through the establishment of cross-functional teams consisting of members from all affected groups. Each cross-functional process should be identified and defined just as any other process, and each one needs an owner as well. Cross-functional teams use the same operating principles and should employ the same systematic approaches to their improvement efforts as other teams. It is important that cross-functional teams rise above parochial issues and concentrate on the common processes they were created to address.

3. *Create special teams for special issues.* Emergent problems within the organization will demand immediate attention. Although they are short-term and take on a problem-solving nature instead of a continuous improvement nature, *special efforts* are every bit as important as ongoing processes and long-term problem solutions. One way of dealing with emergent issues is to create special teams to deal with selected issues and then disband them upon resolution of the issue.

4. *Work toward everyone becoming part of an improvement team.* Individual improvement contributions are important, but it is through team effort in the formal process improvement cycle that individual contributions become "synergized" and larger improvements take place. Every individual in the organization should be part of at least one improvement team, their natural work group. All employees have something to contribute.

Individuals on a team learn to count on and trust other team members and thus become more effective in their own jobs. Optimal team size depends on the extent of the process involved. Many good ideas will come from the workers because they are the closest to the processes where work actually gets done. It is important to create opportunities for them to participate.

5. *Support and reinforce team behavior and performance.* Leaders will have to demonstrate their expectations of team behavior if teams are to achieve maximum performance. This can be done by verbally reinforcing the need to use team operating techniques and by supporting actions that emphasize team behavior. The leader's encouragement, evaluation, and feedback of a team's activities should focus on team-related behavior and performance. Remember, team success also depends on management participation and commitment.

6. *Recognize effort and approach, not just results.* Some improvement efforts will not yield the expected results. In some instances, for example, the principal outcome will be a deeper knowledge of the process instead of immediate measurable improvement. Teams need to be recognized for their adherence to the desired approach and to team behavior, in addition to being recognized for the results they achieve. In general, if the teams adhere to the philosophy and approach of continuous improvement, they will ultimately improve their processes.

7. *Ensure that process improvement teams are linked vertically and horizontally.* Linking teams vertically ensures that lower-level teams will work consistently with the expectations of higher-level teams and that, as a whole, the organization will proceed logically. Linking teams horizontally ensures that joint groups address common problems and that lessons learned in one area may be applied to other areas without duplicating effort. Teams can be linked vertically by ensuring that the leader of one team is a member of a team at the next higher level. Horizontal linking is accomplished through participation on cross-functional and special improvement teams.

PROVIDE SUPPORT, TRAINING, AND EDUCATION

If leaders expect to implement TQM, and further expect employees to follow suit, they must ensure that *adequate time* and *training resources* are available to support the effort. TQM does not depend on additional people or money; rather, it relies on the availability of time for individuals and groups to pursue improvement efforts and on the availability of training and education to develop needed skills and experience in improvement techniques and tools.

While awareness is the way to get the TQM effort moving, *education and training* will help accelerate it dramatically. Provided in the right place at the right time, it allows for the development of needed skills for both the leader and employees. Education and training must be comprehensive, intensive, and unending.

There are several steps that will ensure material support for the people involved in the improvement process:

1. *Make full use of available training and educational resources.* Training is a valuable resource, but it can be costly. Developing tailor-made training approaches is very effective, but it can be time-consuming and expensive. To reduce the costs of education and training, use readily available training materials where appropriate. This includes books, video tapes, classroom instruction, consultant services, and in-house TQM expertise.

2. *Arrange for continuous training and education.* Without training and education, employees cannot grow in knowledge and overall capability. The leader is responsible for promoting both the professional and personal development of the people involved in the effort. This includes making training available to all employees, both individually and in groups, and ensuring that they receive the training when they will have immediate opportunities to use it. Independent training and education should also be encouraged. Training is continuous; it must be performed throughout the life of the continuous improvement process.

3. *Train the managers and supervisors.* Managers and supervisors are the most important sources of training for their employees. Just as the leader is the focal point of the overall effort, managers and supervisors are the focal points for their own organizations. If they are to ensure that their employees are well trained, they must be well trained themselves.

4. *Educate everyone consistently.* The improvement effort requires that every person in the organization be provided a consistent, common level of knowledge about TQM principles, practices, skills, and techniques. The education and training program must be structured to provide this basic knowledge consistently across the board.

5. *Create time for people to address improvement.* If people are expected to pursue the continuous improvement process, they must be provided time for these efforts. Time must be provided for people to be trained, both on the job and in the classroom, because continuous improvement of their knowledge and capabilities is essential. They must also be able to attend group meetings and perform independent activities such as data collection and analysis. They must *not* be required to provide time for improvement at their own expense.

Allowing people to devote time to improvement will make their overall use of time more effective and efficient. Once people begin to see positive change, many will contribute additional effort voluntarily. And as non–value-added tasks are eliminated through process improvement, more time will be available for the continuing improvement effort.

6. *Organize to support improvement.* Organizing people to support the improvement effort makes it easier to provide the necessary resources. If the organization's natural work groups mirror the improvement efforts, group meetings will be easier to arrange and will fit more naturally into the context of job responsibilities. Having groups follow a consistent process improvement methodology will, of itself, eventually establish an approach to work that includes the time necessary for improvement activities and individual and group training.

BUILD TRUST AND RESPECT

Employees who trust their managers and who are trusted and respected in return can help organizations provide superior services or products. Workers have the best, most up-to-date knowledge about how well processes are working, what problems have arisen, and how work can be improved. If their opinions are respected, they will share their knowledge and creativity with management; this is the best way to ensure continuous improvement.

Trust and respect are essential for individual participation. Without an atmosphere that embodies these two elements, employees will not take actions or make recommendations they perceive to be risky. TQM is a process that depends on every person being unafraid to take chances and unworried about risking his or her self-esteem.

When employees do broach ideas, they should be praised; when they identify problems in the process or systems, they should be thanked; when they contribute, they should be recognized; when they fail, they should be supported; and when they succeed, they should be rewarded. The leader is responsible for establishing an atmosphere of trust and support and for maintaining each individual's sense of self-worth and self-esteem.

To establish this type of atmosphere:

1. *Recognize that people are an important treasure.* People are the most important treasure of the organization; they are more than a mere resource. They must not be treated as expendable. They represent experience, knowledge, corporate memory, and the spirit of the organization. In times of hardship, every other alternative must be tried before considering personnel cuts; people are the only element not easily replaceable. In addition to being the lifeblood of the organization, people are the fuel for continuous improvement progress. Every action the leader takes must recognize their importance, and the leader must avoid ever treating them as subordinate to the system.

2. *Value and encourage individual contributions.* Recognition is an essential human need. Every person's sense of self-worth must periodically be affirmed. Recognizing specific individual contributions to the organization or to the improvement effort is the most obvious way of acknowledging an individual's value. By taking an active interest in each person's day-to-day activities, leaders show not only that they care about employee performance, but that they also care about the employees themselves as individuals. Taking prompt actions on their suggestions also shows them that their ideas and contributions to the organization are highly valued.

3. *Recognize that everyone has a responsibility for quality.* People will contribute most when they believe they are responsible for something vital. When the leaders recognize that quality is the responsibility of every individual every day, it becomes easier for them to accept the importance of providing the resources necessary for continuous improvement. Without the time and training necessary to support them, improvement efforts will wither and die. All individuals must have the resources they need to fulfill their personal responsibility for the quality of their processes. By providing these necessary resources, leaders enable the organization to realize its vision of continuous quality improvement.

4. *Listen to even the smallest voice.* Every individual has the potential to contribute to the improvement effort. People are often shy and reluctant to contribute in a group setting, and sometimes that reluctance will be maintained individually as well. The leader must encourage each individual to contribute, utilizing techniques like systematic brainstorming, for example.

Recognizing each contribution (no matter how small), praising ideas publicly, and consulting every individual whenever possible, will help develop a climate in which people are increasingly willing to participate actively in the improvement effort. Even if the ideas elicited seem relatively insignificant, the leader should show enthusiasm and support; a terrific idea can spring from the most unlikely source.

MAKE CONTINUOUS IMPROVEMENT A WAY OF LIFE

If continuous improvement is made a part of the daily routine, it will become integrated into all aspects of work. Continuous improvement only approaches maturity when it is applied *routinely* to all work. Routine application entails using the continuous improvement process in all areas, collecting and using data to assess process suitability, removing roadblocks to the improvement effort, and continuously increasing knowledge and expertise in the improvement process.

Ideally, continuous improvement should be the normal approach to doing work; it must become a way of life.

Here are the steps for making it so:

1. *Expect improvement.* If continuous improvement is truly to become a way of life, improvement should be expected routinely, not only from the leader, but from all employees, peers, and superiors. Expecting improvement does not mean punishing employees when it does not occur; rather it means being *unwill-*

ing to accept the status quo. In a continuous improvement environment, positive change is deliberately sought as the means of engendering improved performance. Questions are continually asked, and measures are made to assess degrees of change. Leaders must constantly demonstrate through actions and words that they are never satisfied with anything less than continuous improvement.

2. *View problems as opportunities.* Identified problems offer the best chance to improve processes. Many individuals tend to see problems negatively, as indications of failure. Instead, emergent or long-term problems should be viewed as golden opportunities. Problems are, in fact, a gold mine of potential savings in personnel, dollars, or time. They signal an opportunity to develop better products or services, created with less effort. Acknowledging problems and rewarding those who bring them to light is an essential part of the continuous improvement effort.

3. *Constantly examine the value of policies, practices, and procedures.* Throughout the organization there will be policies, practices, and procedures that contradict TQM goals and desired behavior. It is important to identify these contradictions, examine their value, and modify them if the TQM effort is to be successful. This is a continuous effort because new policies and practices are always coming into being, and not all will be consistent with TQM. It is important to eliminate those elements that add no value or that demoralize and demotivate individuals within the organization.

4. *Drive out the forces of fear.* Fear causes resistance to change, and fear of the improvement effort will force the expenditure of great amounts of effort that might have been used more productively in actual improvement activities. One main source of fear is the "shoot the messenger" tendency in many organizations.

Don't blame individuals who report problems; those problems are opportunities for improvement that would not otherwise have been discovered. Likewise, do not penalize the individual reporting the problem by making its solution his or her responsibility—unless, of course, he or she "owns" the process with the problem.

Another common individual and group fear is that of survival in a new environment. It is very important to assure individuals and groups that their positions will not be eliminated through their own improvement efforts; although their jobs may change, they must continue to have jobs in the organization.

5. *Recognize success and share the credit.* Recognizing success is another way to reduce fear and to encourage individual and group improvement activity. Recognition is a fundamental human need, and celebration of success is a fun way to provide that recognition in a nonthreatening, noncompetitive environment. Frequent celebrations will demonstrate the leader's interest in all the organization's improvement efforts, help engender feelings of goodwill associated with the improvement process as a whole, and make the workplace more enjoyable.

6. *Assess improvements based on data, not intuition.* Total quality management is about measurement: measurement to assess the need for process improvement, measurement to localize symptoms, measurement to verify causes, and measurement to evaluate changes. It is not possible to reliably determine the course or the success of the improvement effort without collecting and using data effectively. And it is necessary to measure what is important—not what is easy or readily available.

Intuition is valuable in interpreting data and determining future courses of action, but the data themselves validate the improvement methodology and practices. Don't just *think* something is better—*verify it with data*. An experiment is better than an argument.

7. *Encourage innovative thinking and new ideas.* In the spirit of continuous improvement and positive change, it is important to ensure that the organization is receptive to new ways of doing things. Employees are the richest source of improvement ideas. Small, incremental improvement ideas are usually easy to implement, but they need to be approved, encouraged, and acted upon quickly. Prompt action on employee suggestions is more meaningful than tangible rewards.

8. *Align the reward and recognition systems with TQM philosophy.* Reward and recognition systems must be consistent with improvement behavior and attitudes being developed. Implementing continuous improvement will provide continuing opportunities for a constant flow of individual and group rewards and recognition, all of which should be authorized and directed by the TQM leaders and unencumbered by any bureaucratic, centralized system.

Outstanding *group* behavior should always be reinforced and rewarded if possible. When individual behavior is rewarded exclusively, there's always a risk of making one person look good at the expense of the group. Group rewards also reinforce teamwork.

9. *Cease reliance on mass inspection.* Mass inspection is an extremely expensive and unreliable method of ensuring quality. Mere inspection, and discard or rework, does nothing to fix the underlying process problems that cause the deficiencies. More reliable and efficient quality management will be achieved when process controls and improvement are emphasized over inspection. This means shifting focus gradually over the course of the improvement effort until inspection becomes only a means of developing *indicators of process adequacy*.

10. *Justify costs intelligently.* Proposed quality improvements may not always be justified on the basis of their projected financial savings, but they may bring intangible benefits that could far outweigh their immediate monetary costs. So, careful judgment must be exercised when determining the true value of a proposed improvement. Often, large downstream benefits may accrue from an upstream improvement.

It is important, therefore, to examine a potential improvement for both the tangible and intangible benefits it will provide in terms of a better workplace, more satisfied employees, or higher achieved levels of quality. The true cost and savings may, in fact, be unknown and unknowable. It is best, therefore, to implement improvements with the continuous improvement philosophy always in mind.

CONTINUOUSLY IMPROVE ALL PROCESSES

Continuous process improvement, as the basis of TQM and the organization's way of life, is a never-ending effort. Perfection is an ultimate, unattainable goal, but its ideal is the basis for continuous improvement efforts. Everything the organization does must be viewed in terms of interrelated processes. Goals and objectives are realized through process improvement. The focus should be to improve all processes owned and to remove all barriers that hinder others from improving their owned processes. The only true measure of performance over time is the degree of process improvement actually achieved.

Process standardization is a means of defining a process and ensuring that everyone understands and employs it in a consistent manner. It is difficult to improve upon something that is not well defined.

Process standards communicate the current best-known way to perform a process and ensure consistent process performance by a variety of individuals. With a process standard, people have a way to know that they are doing their jobs correctly, and they have a means of assessing their performance objectively. Process standards also provide the baseline from which to continuously improve the process. The people doing the work should maintain and update the standards as they improve their processes, so that the standards always reflect the current best-known means of doing the work.

Here are some steps for continuously improving processes:

1. *Understand what constitutes a process.* TQM focuses on process improvement, so everything the organization does should be described in terms of a process. Simply defined, a process is a transformation of inputs into outputs. Inputs may be materials, money, information, opinions, needs, or anything else a process uses in its transformation. Outputs are products, services, and information. Processes are bounded activities that may be described, and they are often repetitive.

2. *Develop process ownership.* Only a process's owner truly has the power to improve that process. A process owner has both the responsibility for the correct functioning of and the authority to change that process. Having a stake in how well the process functions, the process owner must have as much latitude to change the process as necessary for it to function optimally. That authority enables the owner to pursue the best possible approach to *continuous improvement*. The process owner may be an individual or a team. If an individual owns a process, it will be beneficial to establish a process improvement team or an existing work group as the designated team.

3. *Ensure that every team owns its process.* Just as the leaders must have the authority and ownership over the processes for which they are responsible, teams under their leadership must be *given ownership* over their processes. These teams must have a formal stake in how well the processes work, the responsibility for correct process functioning, and the authority to change their processes where necessary. Without de facto process ownership, team improvement efforts risk being ineffective because of the threat of external reversal of their efforts, or because of a disinterest in the effort as a whole.

4. *Carefully define the processes.* Process definition is an essential prerequisite to process improvement. Teams can't improve what they cannot define. Process definition begins by defining the customer, whether that customer is internal or external to the organization. In addition to defining the customer, it is necessary to define the inputs and outputs, both tangible and intangible, and how to measure them. Finally, the process must be set down in writing, the most common technique being flowcharts or flow diagrams. Until the process can be set down on paper, no one can really understand what that process is or how to measure it.

5. *Study process variation.* A concept that is key to understanding the principles of TQM is *variation* and its effects on how to judge process performance and process capability. Variation is present in every process all the time. What is put into the process, whether it's information or raw materials, varies from day to day, as does what is gotten out of it. Luckily, simple tools are available for understanding, measuring, and reducing variation. The goal is to reduce *sources of variation* as much as possible so processes become more stable and more predictable.

6. *Bring processes under control.* With the knowledge of how to identify and track variation comes the knowledge of how to distinguish between special (assignable) and common (inherent) causes of variation. It is important to identify the special causes that are not endemic to the process itself, such as poor training or power surges, and also the common causes that are variations within the process, such as machine error or material variability. Once the causes of variability are identified, the next step is to work on their removal.

As the special causes of variation are eliminated, the performance of a process will become stable. Variation will still arise from common causes, but it will be predictable within a known range (the control limits). Such a process is said to be in statistical control.

7. *Improve on current process standards.* The process to be improved must be clearly described and readily understood by all individuals who will participate in it. This description, or process standard, should be readily available for reference by all. Constant encouragement is needed for participants to follow the current standard and to improve the process through both group improvement activities and individual initiatives. Process standards should allow for frequent and easy updates.

8. *Assess process capability.* Once the process is in statistical control and all operators are using standard procedures, it will be possible to assess the capability of the process as it is currently structured. If the desired performance levels are different from those being achieved in the stable and controlled process, there is a need for innovation or fundamental changes in the process structure to achieve new performance levels.

9. *Remove process complexity.* Before major changes are considered for the work of an organization, efforts should always be made to simplify and consolidate the organization's processes as much as possible, and to eliminate unnecessary steps. Great savings can be realized by eliminating wasteful effort, and the result is processes that are more productive, efficient, and timely.

The process definition effort will usually uncover many places where the processes can be streamlined. Subsequent process improvement efforts will also identify further simplifications. Only after processes are completely streamlined is it feasible to consider major investments in automation and equipment.

10. *Encourage small incremental improvements.* Incremental improvements are the real backbone of the improvement effort. Although dramatic innovations usually provide the potential for great leaps in capability, their opportunities are relatively rare.

Incremental improvements to existing processes and capabilities are the most practical way to achieve continuous improvement. Therefore, improvement expectations should be framed in moderate, deliberate increments of improvement, not in great leaps forward. The sum of the incremental improvements achieved, both through individual and group activities, will be as impressive as those gained through innovation.

EXPAND THE TQM CULTURE TO SUPPLIERS

The organization's ability to improve its processes depends in part on the inputs to those processes. To the extent that materials and services are procured from other organizations, the continuous improvement effort depends on those suppliers. Expanding the improvement culture to all suppliers will help ensure that the quality of process inputs is sufficient to meet the improvement objectives. This can be done by working more closely with suppliers, helping them to get their own improvement efforts underway, removing roadblocks to an effective acquisition process, building mutual trust and respect, and generally by becoming a better customer for them.

Here's how to involve suppliers in the continuous improvement process:

1. *Simplify the acquisition process.* A complicated, bureaucratic acquisition process irritates suppliers and discourages their participation in the organization's work. Such a process can hide inefficiencies in the overall supply process and is likely to hinder timely procurement of the appropriate materials and services.

By examining the acquisition process and eliminating unnecessary or redundant requirements and procedures, it will be possible to procure needed inputs more effectively and efficiently. Applying TQM to procurement processes is one logical means of simplifying them. The resulting improved process will benefit both the organization and its suppliers.

2. *Involve suppliers early.* Total quality management is a lengthy process requiring years to reach maturity. If an organization waits for its own effort to become mature before involving suppliers, it may be twice as long before purchased materials and service improvements are achieved.

Involving suppliers early will help to reap the maximum benefit from the combined improvement effort as soon as possible. Additionally, involving suppliers early enables both parties to take advantage of lessons learned by the other at times when they are most useful.

3. *Engage suppliers in mutual problem solving.* If suppliers can be encouraged to participate in solving problems affecting both parties, each will benefit from the perspective of the other. Forming joint customer/supplier teams to work on mutual problems is one means of addressing these problems. Such teams are particularly appropriate since the customer and the supplier are joint owners of the acquisition process. These joint teams must work to achieve agreed-upon objectives with the overall goal being to improve the way each business is conducted.

4. *Help suppliers improve.* The best way to improve the quality of procured materials and services is to assist the suppliers in improving their own processes. This can be done by holding supplier TQM seminars, allowing suppliers to attend in-house classes or training sessions, instituting personnel exchange programs, and providing quantitative data to suppliers on their performance. These activities must take place in an unrestricted atmosphere if they are to have substantial effect. The best rule is to treat suppliers as though they are part of your own organization, for in effect they *are* as important a part as the actual members.

5. *Reward suppliers that are improving.* Being recognized for improvement is as important to suppliers as it is to individuals and groups within the customer's organization. Suppliers may be rewarded for demonstrating improvement through reduced oversight of their processes, additional contract awards, pricing or performance preferences, or increased contract profit levels, depending on the organization's acquisition policies and regulations. Suppliers must know that their efforts to improve are recognized and are believed to be important.

6. *Minimize the number of suppliers used.* The increased amount of attention devoted to suppliers in a TQM environment implies that the ideal should be to embark on closer, longer-term partnerships with fewer suppliers. To the extent that such relationships are possible, the organization should restrict its business dealings to only those suppliers with demonstrated TQM enthusiasm and a growing capability. A good policy would be to notify suppliers of this intent and give them the chance to institute or upgrade their own TQM efforts. Ultimately, an organization's improvement objectives will not be attainable unless all suppliers subscribe to the same set of beliefs and practices.

7. *Succeed with the fewest but best suppliers.* Distinguishing among suppliers may be difficult at first. By using an objective set of criteria to evaluate suppliers, it is possible to determine the ones with whom the best long-term relationships can be developed. Key things to look for in a supplier mirror the significant elements of the organization's improvement effort: a vision of continuous process improvement, leadership by top management, a focus on teamwork, and an emphasis on data-driven improvement.

8. *Listen to suppliers.* Being the best customer means listening to the suppliers for a clear, concise reflection of your needs, requirements, and expectations. Suppliers cannot provide the materials and services required unless your requirements have been clearly and explicitly communicated. It must be ascertained that the supplier understands your requirements and is capable of meeting them. Because needs and requirements are never static, listening is an ongoing effort.

9. *Remove roadblocks and barriers.* As with other areas of TQM, one of the most effective contributions customers can make is to remove roadblocks and barriers to effective acquisition processes. In addition to streamlining the processes, the customer should continually evaluate the acquisition efforts to determine the rough spots, especially those created internally. Those that are identified should then be promptly and effectively removed. It is not enough to improve the acquisition process to reduce the time required; it is important to remove all true barriers and non–value-added work efforts.

10. *Work to build mutual trust and respect.* Developing a long-term partnership depends on establishing an atmosphere of mutual trust and respect. Without that trust, efforts to help suppliers develop their own TQM efforts will not be fully accepted; neither will the customer unconditionally accept the suppliers' improvement results. By approaching business negotiations in an open manner, by establishing joint problem-solving efforts, and by offering to share improvement expertise, a great deal of goodwill can be created, and this will provide a foundation for the desired atmosphere of mutual trust and respect.

SUMMARY

These guidelines for the understanding, application, and implementation of the root concepts of TQM have described specific behavior patterns and sets of actions that will enable company managements to effectively achieve the continuous improvement of personal and group performance and to better align and integrate interfunctional quality improvement efforts. They emphasize constancy of purpose, leadership, communication, teamwork, education, statistical thinking, and mutual respect. They focus on customers and promote the integration of suppliers. In essence, they deal with the people-oriented and cultural foundations that really form the basis of how a company actually functions—that is, how it is actually being managed.

Knowledge and acceptance of these root principles of TQM is required before a company can begin to develop its own unique program and start to realize the true potential available from total quality improvement. Implementation can commence in any area at any time, but it must ultimately become companywide. If it takes a heavy investment, and it probably will, it's not because the program is difficult to work. It's because the leaders have been struggling with a less-productive vision, focusing primarily on the pot of gold at the end of the rainbow instead of the productive and personally rewarding journey along the way.

CHAPTER 8

THE TREND TOWARD MANAGEMENT EXCELLENCE

During the transition to companywide quality improvement systems throughout the eighties and the introduction and quick advancement of TQM, leading business executives in the United States began a transformation of their own. Although not as obvious as the overall trends in quality improvement, yet infinitely more meaningful, evidence suggests a slowly evolving conversion to management excellence. Through exposure to and involvement with quality improvement, forward-thinking executives are gradually realizing that quality is indeed a management issue—one vitally dependent on the wholesomeness and direction of management leadership.

A tenet of business holds that real value can be measured in terms of contribution to performance, cost, or schedule—with performance clearly comprising both product or service integrity and customer satisfaction. Quality improvement, therefore, must be of significant business value, because it is directed solely at the maintenance and improvement of overall company performance, an obligation that is customarily associated with the role of management.

Most books on the subject of "management" portray the accomplishment of satisfactory companywide performance as the essence of good management. Theoretically then, quality improvement can be viewed as a dynamic extension of top management's most fundamental role into all areas of company activity. In the right light, this connection can become a practical, business-effective link between the very top and the bottom of an organization.

To further explore this thesis, a true concern repeatedly pondered in the inner offices of top executives who are being challenged to deal with quality improvement has to be: "What is the true business value of *quality*? Is it what its advocates say it is, or is some of it of real value, while the rest is pure hype? Where do we draw the line?"

Many of the answers sensed by these executives must have been inadequate, confusing, or simply unacceptable for them to immediately convert to quality improvement discipleship. As actually perceived, the answer could only have been irrefutably acceptable if it communicated obvious value, that is, if it clearly equated quality improvement activities with business value.

To achieve this important business connection, proposals for companywide quality improvement would have to carefully and indisputably bridge the perceived gap between full customer satisfaction and business economics. Since this did not always happen, many proposals for quality improvement were prone to misinterpretation and fraught with danger, with the danger taking the form of top management being either too restrictive—not allowing the program to flourish as designed—or too trusting—allowing outsiders too much latitude without enough accountability. Thus the stage was set for much that actually happened during the decade of the eighties.

The experience of the eighties also made it clear that most working managers find it at least somewhat difficult to accept outright the tools of quality improvement as a valuable business asset. While they may appreciate the occasional identification of a real problem, they almost never appreciate attempts to influence their own management style and actions. This standard reaction, or resistance, to forthright companywide implementation plans for quality improvement became one more top management challenge in the pursuit of quality progress in America.

As a direct result of these challenges, strengthened by continued worldwide quality competition, some senior executives have found the management courage and personal integrity to stake their future on quality, that is, to lead, fully support, and personally participate in the quality improvement process. These pioneers have reaped the rewards of their faith or daring with increased profits and unexpected growth opportunities. Now, they are being counted among today's successful worldwide competitors. Through their discriminating personal efforts and winning experience, they have learned a new meaning of management excellence, fully realizing that is what has been happening in their companies.

THE PRINCIPLES OF MANAGEMENT EXCELLENCE

The principles of management excellence to be presented here are not all-inclusive; but they have clearly been integral to the achievements of many successful managers, as a direct result of their personal involvement in quality improvement.

Although these principles of conduct may, in fact, differ from those normally found in management textbooks, they do represent, as observed over many years of successful quality management experience, the essential skills that top managers need to achieve true quality improvement. Or vice versa, they represent the kind of management excellence that can result from wholehearted involvement in quality improvement.

Knowledge

The first principle is *knowledge*. Managers who do not intimately know how their functions work and interact with others can never be sure of fulfilling the responsibilities for which they were hired or promoted. Such knowledge includes the detailed needs of internal customers, work-process ownership and standards, cross-functional difficulties, and so forth. The days of managers who have actually participated in almost every job within the organization are long gone. Today's managers have to personally invest in this knowledge if it is to be a factor in their function's performance.

In these highly competitive times, the business value of each company function, perhaps its very survival, depends to a large degree on its ability to satisfy its customers. This ability, in part, depends on the manager's in-depth knowledge of the function and his or her detailed knowledge of the other functions with which interaction takes place. When this personal knowledge is weak or nonexistent, the manager often cannot "be in control" of important business situations. Rather, he or she is at the mercy of others who may or may not be considerate.

Managers who excel today seem to vigorously pursue the kind of detailed company knowledge and intelligence that lets them always be on top of any conceivable situation. In a very short time, knowledge thus gained gives such ambitious managers added abilities and confidence in what would otherwise be a much tougher job.

Part of the knowledge required is a *clear definition of responsibilities*. How many managers have failed because they didn't fully understand their jobs? Their numbers are probably exceeded only by those who have failed because their subordinates, down to the lowest level, did not fully understand their jobs.

A systematic effort to define individual or functional responsibilities in a clear and concise manner is essential to management success. In TQM, this means process definitions. Most working people want to understand their work and to believe in its importance. Without this understanding and belief, they can never feel true pride of accomplishment or grow to fulfill their ultimate capabilities, as envisioned in all programs of quality improvement. A set of clear definitions of responsibility will give any organization added potential.

Management Strength

The next principle of excellence is *management strength*. Managers must have the courage to forge and carry out decisions that are difficult and painful (e.g., having to close down a project or having to say, "We're not ready to start production"). To successfully achieve such strength, managers must:

- Always take a clear, timely, and decisive management position, never sitting back and waiting for the other guy.

- Always provide subordinate personnel with personal and positive support, never leaving them hanging out to dry.
- Always display an eagerness to commit themselves to action.

The initial test of courage for reluctant managers can be rough or, at best, uncomfortable—for example, having to stand up to the company bully or having to take a strong stand on a controversial tissue. But after the first successful ventures, the need for continued, visible displays of strength will diminish. Subordinates and associates will both learn to accept and respect the *new* you; and much wasted time and energy spent in jockeying for position will be purged from the management system.

Consistent displays of courage throughout the management framework of a company will stamp out forever the games people play that tend to plague or sap an organization's ability to progress. And without the quality of personal courage, managers will be hard-pressed to truly lead and convince subordinates of the value of any direction.

Demand for Performance

The third principle of management excellence is an integrated *demand for performance*. When insufficient knowledge exists or there is a lack of clear job or process descriptions, demanding performance may prove to be difficult. For whatever the reason, some managers seem unable to obtain the kind of performance they expect and want from subordinates, and this always results in the most expensive rut an organization can find itself in: a failure to perform up to its capabilities.

To be able to demand performance, a manager must not only be a leader, be honest, and pay a decent wage, he or she must learn to be a just disciplinarian, while personally challenging each subordinate to excel. This approach serves notice to subordinates they can expect to receive fair treatment; and, when religiously carried out, such an approach earns for the aspiring manager the kind of respect that cannot be gained any other way. If quality performance cannot be expected and demanded, it can never happen.

Hand in hand with a demand for performance is *development of people*. While it is readily accepted that the most important component of industry is people, there is no duty more a victim of lip service than the *honest* appraisal and development of human potential. Whatever explanations are cited for this unfortunate situation, they can only be viewed as signs of deficiency or weakness, or simply feeble excuses.

No excuse is acceptable for failure to respond to the development needs of company personnel. Lack of a sufficient and continued effort in the development of people will, in time, turn success into failure. Companywide quality improvement is a natural aid for this duty, providing performance data, customer feedback, and problem-solving situations to learn from. An effective program gives all personnel the opportunity and freedom to learn, contribute, and grow. Imagine what the profits could be, for the company and its employees, if all personnel were honestly developed to their full potential. Aspiring manager, take note.

Strong support for people performance and development will come from *sound relations with others.* Individual organizational segments of a company cannot operate in a void. Each has at least one, but usually several, interfaces with other organizations or individuals, including the end customer. The need to work at having good relations with these associates is fundamental. The primary tools needed for its accomplishment are effective communications, a *strong* and *knowledgeable* management image, and salesmanship.

The true value of favorable interfunctional relations is immeasurable. Its existence will simplify many otherwise difficult tasks, such as uncovering cross-functional problems through the work of quality improvement. There is no better way to create an atmosphere for getting things done than to enjoy and continuously improve interorganizational relations. Essentially, what this really means is knocking down all defensive and parochial fences to become one company family with truly common interests, an absolute must for the *excellent manager.*

The next principles of management excellence are inherent characteristics that, when effectively integrated into the management ambience, spell certain success. These are the principles that distinguish the best from the second best.

Creativity

The first of these principles is *creativity.* There is only slight hope for continued progress without this important characteristic. Although one hears about creativity more frequently in a technological sense, the need for creativity, or innovation if you prefer, exists in every form of human endeavor. Creativity in the *way* businesses are managed (i.e., in management systems) is much needed and can lead to great rewards. For example, a creative approach to quality improvement can lead to excellence in management, increased customer satisfaction, and higher overall productivity.

Creativity is not the exclusive monopoly of a select few. Anyone with a talent for analysis and organized thinking can, by applying this talent to a given objective, realize an innovative idea. Much progress has been accomplished in just this way—think, for example, about the various approaches to quality improvement discussed in this book, each one innovative in its own right.

Loyalty

The second of these more important principles inherent to management excellence is *loyalty.* For many people, this simply means the dedication of years of long hours and faithful service to the company. But the desired meaning of loyalty, and probably the biggest single shortage in the business world today, is much broader. It involves wholehearted faithfulness to the company, to yourself, and to all those for whom you are responsible. It means self-respect and steadfast support for both management and your fellow employees alike. In short, it means *personal integrity*—being true to who you are and what you believe in your heart.

In days gone by, there was an unwritten contract that essentially said 'hat if you do well by the company, the company will do well by you. But this has long since changed. Employees today are generally committed to themselves, to their professions, and, it is hoped, to their work—but *not* to their companies. This unfortunate situation, one of the leading deterrents to business progress, will not change until the managers and leaders of industry themselves embrace and put into practice the deeper meaning of loyalty and personal integrity described above. Managers without this kind of loyalty will not, in the long run, be helping their companies.

Willingness

The last management principle to be discussed is *willingness*, without which there can be no real progress. In an all-emcompassing sense, this means the willingness to *fully accept responsibility*, to *take appropriate risks*, to *learn from experience*, and to *welcome constructive change*—this is the very essence of the job of managers. Willingness of this sort is all-too-rare in management circles today. The more prevalent attitude is one that is parochial and self-centered, which is anathema to quality progress.

It is always easier for managers to do the right things periodically, even if that means to suffer on occasion, than to have the willingness to change their industrial way-of-life to do the right things all the time. Willingness means breaking out of the molds of familiarity and security to become free and to *grow*. Companies need to develop managers who understand and embody willingness— that is, managers who are willing to stand up for *what is right* and to speak out, when challenged, in defense of *quality, integrity,* and *value*.

SUMMARY

Organizations should pursue these fundamental principles of the *quality of management* (see Figure 8–1) as ambitiously and forcefully as they do markets and cost reductions now. Without an organizational plan for management improvement, superior management will never be achieved. But the plan must be correctly conceived and developed.

FIGURE 8-1
The Principles of Management Excellence

Knowledge—Knowing the details of work responsibilities
Strength—Managing with courage
Demand for performance—Causing people to grow
Creativity—Fostering innovative ideas
Loyalty—Leading with personal integrity
Willingness—Doing the right things all the time

What's needed as an essential ingredient for the management plan is a dynamic and relentless pursuit of quality improvement. Implementing the continuous improvement process, more than anything else, will be a catalyst for moving managements in the direction of excellence.

If the *natural* growth of management was already in this direction, rather than toward hidden or selfish agendas, the pursuit of quality improvement would not be a concern. It would already be thoroughly ingrained in the management woodwork. What a great way for an organization to be at peace with itself, its employees, its customers, and, as appropriate, its stockholders!

PART 2—CONCLUSION

In Part 2, we've examined the highlights of TQM; we've explored the central idea of quality improvement; we've carefully walked through the basic elements of implementation; and we then related all of this to the *quality of management*. If this isn't enough to convince good managements of the opportunities to get better, and struggling managements of the opportunity to survive and prosper, let's look at it from a completely different perspective.

Let's look at what the news media publicizes as prominent management ills, for example:

- Management greed and indifference, as represented by the recent rash of illegal actions on Wall Street and the savings and loan crisis.
- Political corruption and incompetence, as represented by the frequently reported high cost overruns of the U.S. Department of Defense and major construction projects.
- The escalating costs of health care, education, and insurance.
- The excessive bureaucratic layers of management.
- The growing gap between the highest and lowest salaries.

Of course, there can be no guarantee that long-term quality improvement would have *prevented* the individual problems represented by these general examples. But try to imagine how different each situation *might have been* if the organizations involved had truly incorporated all the working elements of quality improvement into their operations from top to bottom. These include ingrained disciplines like:

- The clear establishment and enforcement of quality standards for all functions and all personnel.
- The required involvement of customers and suppliers in the establishment of quality standards.
- The initiation and verification of open and honest communications.

- The measurement of performance against the standards, and the awareness of ongoing performance trends.
- The focus on internal and external customer satisfaction.
- The creative involvement of all personnel in the improvement process as individuals and as teams.
- Cost-of-quality and corrective action subsystems.
- The foundation of mutual trust and respect throughout the entire organization and its customers and suppliers.

If the organizations involved in the news-reported situations had believed in and pursued quality improvement, at the very least several individuals would have had the opportunity to *prevent or seriously challenge* either the plans or the individuals involved in the primary actions that led to the reported problems.

Quality improvement systems are like that. Religiously enforced, they can prevent powerful but selfish executives from setting the direction of management conduct on paths that will ultimately lead to the undoing of their organizations. Some current situations may not be immediately reversible, having become much too ingrained over the course of many years. In these cases, the only hope for the future is to begin the long-term process of constructive change: quality improvement.

The Japanese have a clear *vision of quality* and they are truly committed to it. We are surely not able to compete when we settle for anything less. But even when we develop a *passion for quality,* we must be aware that if part of the world has gotten ahead of us, there is no way to catch up overnight. If America's responsive quality improvement efforts aren't long-range and incremental, they just won't happen. And if the necessary investment is lacking, we may stay in the race but, at best, we'll be holding up the rear.

PART 3

IMPLEMENTING AND SUSTAINING THE IMPROVEMENT PROCESS

CHAPTER 9

PREPARING FOR IMPLEMENTATION

In light of the up-front, long-term commitment necessary to meet quality improvement's lifelong challenge, *how* a company begins its quality crusade is crucial. Logic demands that it be well thought-out and right the first time. Getting off to a fast start is not nearly as important as getting off to a good start. Critics of the movement toward companywide quality improvement credit poor implementation plans and execution as primary reasons for failure, whether the movement's leaders be outside consultants or internal advocates.

PRECAUTIONS

There are three major symptoms of *impending failure* to watch for. The first can be called "the promise versus the reality." Advocates often have lots of enthusiasm for the promised results, with little or no realization of the hard work needed to get there. The second symptom is an ingrained pessimistic attitude. Leaders need urgent reminders that the real goal at the beginning is to *get ready* and not to *get it over with*. The third symptom is an insidious bad habit that often causes stagnancy in industrial organizations—a parochial response that powerful company functions feel they have the right to apply to all mandated programs not of their initiation. It can be called "pledge of allegiance versus active participation."

Before finalizing a decision to begin, the decision maker must understand that this is a total company endeavor involving all employees, suppliers, and customers, and that once started there is no turning back. Quality can't be turned on and off like field trials. Once employees and customers experience the taste of real quality improvement, and are able to relish its true worth for themselves and their organizations, they will become preconditioned to personally react to any future reversals. This is one of the many intangible benefits to be derived from *the journey*.

Also before finalizing a decision to begin, the decision maker must be aware of the cost and have the initial resources available. TQM is not cheap. Time is needed to think, to plan, to educate, to train, and to implement; the right tools are needed; hard facts about where you really stand with your customers and other performance measurements are needed; the organizing and support team is needed. These all cost money, and this is definitely not the time to skimp on resources. If you're not convinced of the payback, you probably shouldn't be starting.

Last, but not least, the decision maker should be aware of some known pitfalls to be avoided prior to program start. The following is a collection of obstacles actually experienced in the pursuit of quality progress:

1. Misunderstanding the meaning of *quality*.
2. Entering with reservations—"I believe in the principles, but . . ."
3. Believing quality management means less output.
4. Evaluating cost on a short-term basis.
5. Emphasizing job limitations more than process.
6. Lacking vision—allowing daily routines to interfere with the acceptance of new objectives.
7. Choosing between two alternatives with real knowledge of only one.
8. Taking suspected problem causes for granted rather than checking them out.
9. Overlooking the little things in favor of miracle solutions.
10. Resisting change, as reflected in the following statements:
    - "My people already spend too much time on mandated programs."
    - "We don't have enough people to do this."
    - "I know what my problems are."
    - "My people won't accept this."
    - "My boss doesn't really support this."

Full implementation of the quality improvement process, especially for a large company, will appear as a very large undertaking, even when the cultural environment is right for this beginning. In fact, it *is* a giant task, but it doesn't have to happen all at once.

Rushing into full implementation without carefully preparing a solid foundation for an organized evolution has proven to be a formula for failure for CWQI programs in general. Therefore, even though *companywide* must remain the stated objective from the start, it is often wise to begin in a more manageable pilot area, with a secondary objective to achieve the following:

1. Prove the ability of the *improvement process* to produce cost-effective results.
2. Limit the initial scope of support effort needed.
3. Discover and solve problems unique to the company (e.g., language, conflicting policies, general attitudes, levels of tolerance, lack of discipline, and so forth) prior to a major movement toward full implementation.

GETTING STARTED

Selection of the starting area should be strongly influenced by the size of the opportunity to produce quick and significant results. Depending on the actual situation, it is usually advisable to start with a single department or subunit within the company or an entire small facility in a multifacility company. There are no hard-and-fast rules, but the unit selected should be typical of the company's unique mores of management. And it also helps to have an ambitiously cooperative unit manager.

In one medium-size manufacturing company, the personnel director, a young ambitious executive, was anxious to be selected to pioneer the pilot run for quality improvement. He recognized the value of quality improvement to the company, but more specifically, he saw that, if successful, the improved atmosphere created would make his job a lot easier. This indeed did happen because quality improvement is a people program. But this young executive was surprised by the actual extent of the improvement opportunities he found in his own handling of employee relations and labor relations, most of which arose as a result of his significant attitude change in the job of "listening."

This personnel director's biggest surprise, however, involved the operation of the cafeteria. Everything that was done to improve the quality of the food service not only paid off in customer satisfaction, efficiency, and cost, it also had a great impact on employee morale. Significant improvements in food quality and a changed quality atmosphere in the cafeteria resulted in a new pattern of employee behavior. It became common for employees to leave from lunch well satisfied and to carry this good feeling back to their workstations.

In essence, the success or failure of the initial quality improvement effort will greatly affect the company's willingness to integrate quality improvement ideas into the woodwork of day-to-day operations in all areas. It pays, therefore, to choose these early efforts carefully, looking for opportunities that:

- Have an excellent chance for success.
- Are visible throughout the company and to external customers.
- Can significantly improve the lives of workers and managers alike.

The trick is to find something that is neither so large that the project is doomed to failure, nor so small that no one will notice if improvements are made.

In the light of the criticality of this initial decision, the following recommendations are presented as a guide:

1. *Focus on operations that affect critical issues that are also important to customers.* Addressing critical problem areas increases the chance that quality improvement results will sell themselves. It is then possible to build on early successes to mobilize the majority of the people in an organization. Tangible successes will be much more meaningful than verbal promises. Choosing the right area to start will maximize the initial payback and increase the attractiveness of quality improvement to the entire organization.

2. *Start with the pilot organization's own processes.* Continuous improvement will ultimately involve each individual and group within the entire organization. But beginning the effort within the pilot leader's own span of control provides the easiest opportunity for immediate, visible success—without threatening anyone else's domain. The achievement of such an early success will not only confirm that the improvement process works, it also allows the pioneering group to *demonstrate* the ideals and behavior the company seeks to inspire in others.

3. *Start the improvement process under the direction and leadership of the highest organizational level possible.* If the leader of the initial effort is not the top leader in the company, he or she must promote the promise of quality improvement to the highest audience that can be reached, seeking and confirming, at the very least, their interest and support.

Ideally, the improvement effort is sponsored at the very top of the company. This may not always be possible, however; the improvement process may have to begin at some other point in the organization, that point becoming the top of the implementation by default. At this starting point, the leader must be given a great deal of latitude in determining the overall direction of the effort—so long as this direction is also consistent with broader organizational goals that have been independently communicated.

4. *Cascade the process through the pilot organization.* Once the improvement process has been successfully introduced at the highest possible level, it should then be cascaded sequentially through the organization, area by area, ensuring at each step a complete and thorough understanding and acceptance of the improvement philosophy. It is not necessary to complete the implementation in one area before proceeding to the next, but it is important to ensure that key people are trained and ready. Skipping areas is a crucial mistake because not only will the opportunity for improvement be missed in those areas, there is a sure risk of alienating or threatening those area managers and turning them against the improvement effort.

5. *Predetermine early success levels.* Essentially, a quality improvement program is successful if the level of quality performance is better today than last wcck, or better this year than last year. Once determining the desired status of performance for the initial and subsequent key areas, top management will be able to gauge the progress of the quality improvement effort. Their initial expectations will often be an easily measurable and attainable plateau of improvement, such as a 10 percent reduction in identified errors.

Taking the time to predetermine early and agreeable measures of success can potentially lock in genuine executive interest and support for the crucial early days of implementation. Discussions of potential success levels can also provide a unique opportunity for the leader/advocate to nurture a long-term vision of quality for the company—a vision of transition from where the operation stands today in quality performance, to where it can, should, and will be in the future.

BEING AWARE OF FALSE IMPRESSIONS AND CLEAR SIGNALS

Before starting the implementation, no matter what the plan, don't underestimate the inherent value of the involved management's understanding, interest, and support to the success of the program, or be prepared to join the ranks of those who have tried but failed. All involved management personnel must know how the program operates and fits into the current management scheme of things and understand the basic principles upon which its value rests before taking any step toward implementation.

It is not enough to sell the chief executive. The program will not work by edict. Most managers understandably feel that better quality is like motherhood and the flag; no one opposes it. Therefore, it's easy for them to pledge allegiance to the boss's latest project. But, it takes much, much more; it takes real understanding and acceptance to have hope for a personal buy-in to the efforts required.

It is not uncommon for quality management consultants to receive a phone call that goes something like this: "My boss has decided to go ahead with a quality improvement program, and he wants me to find someone who can tell us exactly what we have to do, to train our people, and to start right now." Inquiries into long-range strategies and specific improvement goals are usually unanswerable, except in general terms. This is a crime! By edict alone, companies are known to have spent considerable sums on formal quality training without ever knowing exactly where they were going or without preparing their management personnel for the golden opportunity that quality improvement truly offers.

A quality improvement system *cannot* compensate for deficiencies in management. If a census could be taken of successes and failures to implement an effective quality improvement system, it would probably show the degree of success achieved to be more dependent on the beginning attitudes of management than on the exact approach taken. The real killer attitudes appear at both ends of the spectrum, where managers either:

1. Do not believe in the program and merely give it lip service.
2. Are so convinced of its value they expect the program to produce miracles, such as compensating for obvious management deficiencies.

An effective quality improvement system can take a good management organization and make it better, but it cannot take an organization of incompetent managers and make them good.

On the other hand, even when top managements are convinced of the potential value of quality improvement, and they have an open and positive attitude about implementation, they must learn to recognize and deal with varying actual conditions of poor quality attitudes throughout the entire organization, conditions that will negatively affect the improvement effort. Common symptoms of an unhealthy quality attitude include:

- Employee comments and complaints being ignored or passed over lightly.
- Employees at all levels generally not taking formal company requirements seriously.
- Company processes (direct and support) being inadequately defined and loosely interpreted.
- Interfunctional problems either being ignored or tolerated without apparent concern.
- Numerous complaints being made about the adequacy and worth of support tools, equipment, and supplies.
- Unhappy and turned-off employees having no real opportunity to speak out and be heard.

These symptoms of an unhealthy quality attitude, some of them fostered by the managers themselves, clearly represent a series of management deficiencies. Their existence within an organization is evidence of a ready opportunity for quality improvement, and they need to be specifically addressed in the implementation plan. Don't miss these signals!

THE QUALITY COUNCIL

Appointment of a quality council, or steering committee, by the executive in charge is one way to offset some degree of expected management problems, regardless of the initial scope of implementation. Passing the baton of quality improvement to a quality council is a transfer of the quality program work tasks and companywide direction, not a transfer of the responsibility for executive leadership. Therefore, the quality council, when utilized, should be composed of the same senior managers who are now entrusted to lead and manage major company functions, those individuals whose decisions and ideas truly make the company what it is today. Without clear direction and authority from this level of management, quality improvement implementation could become an impossible mission.

Typical duties for a quality council are listed here.

1. Determine *what* must be done to implement the companywide quality improvement process and direct the actions and the pace of action necessary for ongoing progress. Begin by deciding the company-unique improvement process to be utilized, choosing the starting area, assigning the start-up team, and funding the start-up effort. Follow-up actions are periodically determined from the inputs of the membership, the proposals of the quality professional, and the recommendations of assigned task teams.

2. Determine *who* is responsible for carrying out the actions decided by the council. Authorize and direct individual or group actions to be executed, after first resolving any budget problems that may be indicated.

3. Provide a communication link between the various functions and units involved in the quality improvement process to ensure that everyone is getting the same word and remains true to the course being developed.

4. Establish ownership for all cross-functional processes and assign cross-functional process improvement teams, as incrementally required.

5. Identify and resolve all major difficulties that may develop as obstacles to quality progress, as determined through council discussion and agreement. For this purpose, identify and assign required quality task teams as follows:

    a. Special task teams to investigate and resolve emergent problems or unusual opportunities demanding immediate attention.

    b. Cross-functional task teams to investigate and resolve cross-functional quality problems or opportunities, leading to the assignment of a standing, cross-functional process improvement team.

Proper use of special task teams can provide unique growth opportunities for select individuals to demonstrate their abilities to take on tough new assignments, to work effectively with assignees from other functions, and to produce results useful to the progress of the company. Normally, these task teams will be composed of representatives from three or more functions. They will have a specific charge, a target date for completion, and a requirement for both a written and an oral report. Once completing their task, they are disbanded forever. When task teams are managed in this way and then complimented with effective recognition, future selection of team membership is a snap, with the best and the brightest anxious to be assigned.

Selecting the chairman for the quality council is another important decision to be made by the executive leader of the program. Active participation in quality council activities is essential for each member, but it is crucial for the chairman, who must not only control the meetings but also keep the long-range aims of quality improvement in the forefront. If the selection isn't an obvious one, the following three criteria are suggested as having worked effectively in specific cases.

1. Pick the senior manager who is most sold on the genuine worth of the program, and let his or her enthusiasm rub off on the others.
2. Pick the senior manager who is most turned off at the outset, effectively forcing him or her to have to *get with it.*
3. Pick the senior manager who has the best working relationship with the quality professional, a liaison important to the success of the program.

The principal reason for the success of one quality council experience was the establishment of rules for the formal conduct of council activities. First, a task team was never allowed to become just another committee. Second, the quality council never scheduled a meeting unless these conditions were met:

- A decision had to be made.
- All pertinent data regarding the decision were available to each council member at least seven working days prior to the meeting date. This allowed council members to hold preparatory discussions with their organization prior to the meeting.
- All meetings were to begin on time and never exceed one and a half hours.

These simple rules, when carried out religiously, created a businesslike atmosphere for the top management work of quality improvement. This, in turn, helped to capture and maintain the interest of the senior managers, thus allowing the business of quality improvement to proceed smoothly and effectively. Of course, the behind-the-scenes planning and organization it took to achieve the above required the services of a professional quality executive, the next subject.

THE ROLE OF THE QUALITY PROFESSIONAL

Although the ongoing management of the quality improvement program remains the responsibility of the quality council or the program's leader/advocate, utilization of a professional quality executive can make the entire effort run more smoothly. The quality professional can help crystalize the exact meaning of quality for each functional area and provide some of the grass-roots leadership and day-to-day guidance and support necessary to keep the entire program on track. It is difficult to imagine the implementation and effective management of a companywide quality improvement program without the benefit of a quality improvement specialist.

What's needed today is what might be termed a *new-breed* quality professional—one who knows what has to be done, has expertise in the tools of quality improvement, is uniquely experienced in the company's business, and is now or has the potential to become a respected member of the top management team. Nothing less will suffice in today's fiercely competitive marketplace. This new quality executive will be operating from a different set of signals than the more familiar, traditional role, working primarily on the discovery and future prevention of quality deficiencies in all company operations. This new role can be viewed as a combination of chief salesperson, quality system educator, facilitator of quality improvement, and promoter of quality strategies.

In acting as the chief salesperson and outspoken champion for quality improvement, the specialist does not take away that responsibility from the executive leader who has made the decision to proceed in the first place. Rather, he or she shares the role, with the leader by bringing it down into the trenches of everyday operations on a full-time basis. This involves finding the proper quality vocabulary to use so that everyone can understand the new company quality system. Since each function has its own peculiar language, this jargon must find its way into ongoing quality communications if all functions are to fully understand and accept the program.

Experience clearly dictates that selling all of management on the true value of quality, and keeping them sold, remains the biggest challenge to most quality professionals. For this reason, the quality professional cannot afford to miss a single opportunity to sell quality. This means endorsing quality not only during the marketing effort needed to start the new program, but also in each and every education or training session, in each management meeting attended, and in each document bearing a quality function signature. The challenge of changing old, well-entrenched views on the meaning of quality demands nothing less. To help with this challenge, the quality executive can learn from the marketing professionals, who might suggest useful hints like the following:

1. Constantly stress user benefits—in other words, always remind employees, from the bottom to the top of the organizational ladder, that quality improvement means customer satisfaction, happy employees, and reduced costs. And always be ready to develop a path from the subject at hand to any one or all of these essential benefits.

2. Always recognize the difference between quality and other functional viewpoints and be prepared to articulate and support your claims for quality. If established quality standards are realistic, you can easily defend the quality viewpoint. If the standards are questionable, you may need to promote the quality maxim "Do it like the requirement or change the requirement to what we and our customers really need."

3. Forget the bad news messages that are so common in traditional quality programs. Always emphasize the good performance that constantly has the potential to be better.

The quality professional's role as quality system educator means being accountable for the development of the quality education and training required for all personnel. Whenever quality improvement has not been an integral part of company operations, its introduction requires a series of educational and training programs for each element of organization as they become involved. Educating all levels of working people to respond differently to quality is not a task to be taken lightly. Basic attitudes about work and mind-sets that have developed over many years are involved. Essentially, this task is aimed at the conversion of all personnel to the value of customer satisfaction and quality disciplines as an integral part of all work.

Being a facilitator for quality improvement is the star role for the quality professional. It goes beyond selling and educating. It, in effect, transcends all other duties. Facilitating is a buzzword heard a lot these days, but it really fits the role of the new-breed quality professional like a glove. It means facilitating the control of quality and the improvement of quality performance in all areas of company operation. The quality professional isn't responsible to design, sell, buy, or produce a product or service for the company, nor to provide direct support to any of these functions. His or her only reason for being is to help others do their jobs better. What better way than facilitating, which means "making things easier"—or in this application, "making quality progress easy." This key role also helps to prevent the quality organization from ever becoming more than a small influence group.

On the ITT corporate quality staff, as on many corporate staffs, the quality professionals didn't have the authority to make company units do things. But they did have the opportunity to offer help to the units—that is, to educate and convince them about how to do their work more productively and less costly while, at the same time, increasing customer satisfaction. It was always rewarding when a positive response was received—and a series of exactly such positive responses over the years helped ITT to achieve some portion of its success.

Strategic planning for quality is another idea whose time has come. Unless the concepts of quality, as discussed in this book, are truly built into all company actions from the first concept of a new product or service to the ultimate satisfaction of its users, all of which may take a year or more, a company cannot be truly confident about the actual cost of this new business offering or the degree of customer satisfaction that will be achieved.

With knowledge gained from daily experiences of quality improvement, the quality professional is in an excellent position to bring quality "realities" to the strategic planning table, asking the hard questions that might otherwise be ignored in the glow of the latest marketing expectations. One key point for quality that must be brought out in the strategic planning process is that if the company cannot compete head-on in quality, with regard to any of its product or service offerings, it must come to grips with this reality, or it must find a niche where competition is possible.

In addition to the duties already described, the quality professional should be able to provide a clear vision of the quality improvement journey contemplated for the company. This could involve a course of transition from where the company is today in quality achievements to where it desires and intends to be in the future.

Besides being able to meet the functional challenges previously discussed, the quality executive should possess certain personality traits. All the following personal characteristics have been known to enhance the effectiveness of senior quality executives:

- *Integrity.* They must epitomize honesty and reliability.
- *Ability to communicate.* They need the skill and courage to communicate orally and in writing that which is not always pleasing to the recipient.
- *Salesmanship.* They must have the ability to sell or influence people to make necessary personal changes or conversions.
- *Curiosity.* They should be instinctively curious about dubious individual actions and exaggerated variations in work practices.
- *Strong human interest.* They should be interested in why people make errors and perform below their capabilities.
- *Factual orientation.* They should always deal in facts rather than opinions, especially avoiding those "facts" established by management fiat.

If all this sounds like some kind of superperson, that's because this is not a job for the weak or timid. Years ago, quality professionals felt good if the company's chief executive supported them. Today, the chief executives urgently need them. But today's professionals must be prepared for today's challenges. They must be knowledgeable about the business of the company as well as competent in using the quality disciplines and tools that are needed.

Today's challenge to the quality professionals is to become like the corporation lawyers whose advice is always heeded. Companies quickly learn that if they don't understand and follow the law, they can get into big trouble. In exactly the same way, companies are now learning that if they don't build quality into all operations, they will sooner or later get into big trouble in the marketplace. For today's quality professionals, this is their golden opportunity.

CHAPTER 10

SUSTAINING QUALITY IMPROVEMENT PROGRESS

Realizing that quality improvement is not a quick-fix solution for the company's ills but rather a permanent "way of life" makes it logical to avoid rushing into a false start. Management should seek all the staying power possible for the improvement program. Roadblocks can and will occur, initially and periodically throughout the journey. It is a function of people's natural resistance to change. Therefore, it is reasonable to supplement the improvement effort with formal activities, from time to time, that have the power to sustain or renew interest in continued higher levels of performance.

REVISITING THE COMPONENTS OF THE SYSTEM

Until continuous quality improvement becomes an integral part of the woodwork of the company's management system, actions to sustain progress will always be useful, starting with revisiting the business culture components of the central quality system.

The *communications* system offers unlimited opportunities to generate and publicize interest-sustaining and motivating messages. For example, management can:

- Display updated information on graphs comparing performance to objectives so that employees can track progress.

- Make periodic use of banners or posters with graphic reminders like "What have you done for your customer lately?"

- Hold periodic group meetings to discuss quality progress, potential problems, and new opportunities.

- Sponsor messages that reemphasize their vision of quality's role in the business, publicize recent outstanding achievements, and promote and stimulate the idea of "staying the course."

The *education* system is sustaining progress whenever it orients and trains newcomers, retrains current employees as the system changes, or offers new, advanced courses for personal proficiency on subjects like innovations, teamwork, and risk taking.

The *recognition* system, as previously stated, remains the most important avenue for sustaining interest and commitment to quality progress. Each time an individual or group is newly recognized, their personal enthusiasm is bound to grow—and to rub off on others.

SPECIFIC SUSTAINING EFFORTS

In addition to revisiting communications, education, and recognition, there are other, more exclusive ways to stimulate continued progress. Your quality professional should be able to provide specific recommendations and fill in the details for applicable portions of the following sustaining efforts.

Self-help employee participation programs are available in the marketplace—including the Japanese import, quality circles. They all have value so long as they do not represent the main course. They are supplementary to the overall improvement program, designed to support and sustain the ongoing process in specific organizations where they may be suitable and beneficial. Be aware of these programs. Use them from time to time as appropriate and desirable to the betterment and continuance of quality improvement activities in particular segments of the organization.

A *quality system audit* is a tool used by manufacturing companies to periodically determine how effectively their product quality control system is functioning. A similar approach could be taken to periodically assess how well the companywide quality improvement system is functioning. The quality improvement activity that most closely resembles a quality audit is the original assessment of process and job specifications, quality responsibilities, standards, and measurements. That initial effort could easily be considered a quality system audit, and it wouldn't be a bad idea to periodically recreate or requalify the system foundation—but only after it has been fully implemented for at least a couple years. A company should consider auditing its quality improvement system only after all functions agree that it really is and has been working. Once agreed, schedule the audit on a two- or three-year cycle, and organize it to have a different functional manager in charge each time.

Strategic quality planning is the formal integration of quality into the strategic planning process. Its use will add substance to the strategic plans of any company—and it will permit quality to become and remain a proactive rather than a reactive component of the corporate planning process.

When properly integrated into the business plan, quality performance can be used to support both marketing projections and operations cost budgeting. The key to its use for strategic planning is to include quality performance knowledge in the planning process, for example, requiring key functions to:

- Relate plan-year performance commitments to current, actual performance capabilities.

- Establish specific functional quality performance improvement objectives for the plan-year.

- Integrate these quality facts into the business plan.

To accomplish this kind of planning, a company must have valid knowledge of quality performance, the kind that can only come from a viable system of performance measurement and improvement. The major contribution of this knowledge is to provide greater credibility to the business planning process, because it takes the guesswork and unjustified optimism out of performance assumptions. With valid quality performance information, a company can be assured, as much as possible, that it won't have any big performance surprises in the plan-year—surprises that might otherwise wipe out a major portion of the plan's expected results.

PART 3—CONCLUSION

It is clear that starting quality improvement slowly, carefully, and incrementally is the right way to avoid implementation problems or early termination. Permanent and dramatic change is what's needed, and that won't happen overnight. So don't be afraid to start small and then let the improvement system sell itself—that is, let it grow *naturally*.

Once started, companywide quality improvement should sustain itself. It certainly has the potential to interest and excite all involved, and to be a dynamic force against the status quo. But if it does falter in any area, management can rejuvenate it with some of the ideas expressed in this section.

OVERALL CONCLUSION

This book has attempted to examine the quality improvement efforts of the eighties and to identify those events that are most likely to be of significance in business advances of the nineties and beyond. It has portrayed companywide focus on people, work processes, and quality standards as the prime substance of breakthrough progress in both manufacturing and service organizations, significantly enhanced by the participative integration of management, employees, customers, and suppliers.

Looking forward to effective utilization of this knowledge, the book briefly described total quality management as representing the height of accomplishment. Then after examining the central idea of TQM, it presented detailed guidelines on how to achieve the promised results. The improvement process was likened to an organized gravitation to *management excellence,* and the overall treatise was then supplemented with suggestions for implementing and sustaining quality progress.

Although individual elements of the entire mission of quality improvement may now appear to make good business sense, taken together they become a mammoth project—one that will require a long-term commitment, a significant up-front investment, and courage of the first order. But if this book has successfully shown the value of quality improvement at all stages of a company's operations, readers will strongly believe that *this is the path American industry must follow.*

U.S. businesses as a whole have taken a backseat to the new economic leaders of the world, and a lot of what has been discussed in this book is at the heart of this unfortunate but unmistakable trend—a trend that most business, government, and academic leaders would love to reverse. As a result, we see and hear a lot of uproar about this deteriorating condition, many different ideas about what to do, a revolving level of confidence, challenges from all quarters, and so on—but *no real plan.*

In addition to being relegated to second-class world-business citizenship, U.S. businesses are frequently accused of being seriously lacking in ethics and compassion—that is, being excessively dominated by materialism and greed, a condition that slowly but surely destroys moral values, human rights, and fidelity in business relationships. The bad news is that guilty verdicts are being confirmed every day by the news media.

On the basis of its loss of both economic leadership and strong ethical standards, we could easily judge U.S. business to be in a state of decay, very much in need of a prescription for survival. But where is that prescription?

It is right here between the covers of this book. It's exactly what you have been reading about. If you have been paying attention, the message should be clear. It may also be disturbing, or at least discomforting—but it is reality. It does not call for some kind of magic. It calls for everyone to just do what they're supposed to do, and to love doing it.

Will American Industry do it? Will we each light our candle to help overcome the darkness of the past? Where do we find inspiration and hope to help us make a deep personal investment in the future?

Is it with the government? No, the government seems hopelessly out of touch with the real business and economic needs of our country, failing to make even a small dent in the national debt.

Is it with the business leaders who have brought this condition about, or with those follow-up leaders they have mentored? No, these people are giving us exported jobs, ruthless belt-tightening, lip service about quality improvement, and higher executive pay. Their motto seems to be, "get the quick-and-dirty profits, at any risk to all but ourselves;" and that "all" includes those of us who depend on them for our futures.

Is it with the academic leaders of our country? No, the MBAs of the eighties and nineties, so far, seem to have fallen right in step with the ongoing trend of business failing to benefit society. Certainly, they have not brought with them any obvious new thoughts on the subjects of integrity, compassion, and long-term business planning.

Is it with the boards of directors of our corporations? Perhaps—but only if they can find their courage. As the number of major business failures continues to mount, boards of directors are more and more being maligned as "gutless rubber stamps for management." On the other side of this coin, if the boards could see the real value of quality improvement—and have the management strength to act in a positive, demanding way—they could not only prevent future business failures, they could make a major contribution to the future of America.

Is it with those exceptional leaders who have pioneered real quality improvement and proved, once again, that America can compete? Yes! Thanks to these brave individuals who have brought us order-of-magnitude improvements in every aspect of running a business, we *do* have the answer for a happy future. The answer is *total quality management*—fully understood, fully believed in, and fully integrated over time into all business practices of American industry.

ENDNOTES

CHAPTER 1

The Trend toward Companywide Quality Systems

1. Material in this chapter is excerpted from *BBP Handbook of Quality Management*, 1992. Copyrighted material reprinted with permission of BBP HANDBOOK OF QUALITY MANAGEMENT and Bureau of Business Practice, 24 Rope Ferry Road, Waterford, CT 06386.
2. Material in this paragraph is excerpted by permission from J. Ryan, "Is U.S. Quality Competitiveness Back?" *Quality Progress*, December 1989, pp. 37–39.
3. Material in this subsection (two paragraphs) is excerpted by permission from N. Karabatsos, "Quality in Transition—Part One," *Quality Progress*, December 1989, pp. 22–26.
4. Material in this subsection (two paragraphs) is excerpted by permission from L. P. Sullivan, "The Seven Stages in Companywide Quality Control," *Quality Progress*, May 1986, pp. 77–83.
5. For an up-to-date discussion of product quality control, refer to the following ASQC Quality Press books: J. B. Keats and D. C. Montgomery (eds.), *Statistical Process Control in Manufacturing* (1991); D. C. Brauer and J. Cesarone, *Total Manufacturing Assurance: Controlling Product, Reliability, Safety, and Quality* (1991); and I. L. Bare and B. Bare, *The Self-instructional Route to Statistical Process Control and Just-in-Time Manufacturing* (1991).
6. For a more complete discussion of this subject, refer to the following ASQC Quality Press books: R. J. Pierce (ed.), *Leadership, Perspective, and Restructuring for Total Quality* (1991); and F. C. Collins, Jr., *Quality: The Ball in Your Court* (1991).
7. Material in this subsection (two paragraphs) is excerpted by permission from W. J. McCabe, "Examining Processes Improves Operations," *Quality Progress*, July 1989, pp. 26–32.
8. Material in this subsection (two paragraphs) is excerpted by permission from E. H. Melan, "Process Management in Service and Administrative Operations," *Quality Progress*, June 1985, pp. 52–59).

9. For a more complete discussion of this subject, refer to the following ASQC Quality Press books: R. H. Slater, *Integrated Process Management: A Quality Model* (1991); H. J. Harrington, *Business Process Improvement—A Way to World Class Status* (1991); and G. Fellers, *SPC for Practitioners: Special Cases and Continuous Processes* (1991).

CHAPTER 2

The Responsibilities for Quality

1. Material in this subsection (three paragraphs) is excerpted from G. J. Kidd, Jr., "What Quality Means to an R&D Organization," ASQC Quality Congress, 1987. Reprinted with the permission of ASQC.
2. For a sampling of the many available design quality tools, refer to the following ASQC Quality Press books: T. B. Barker, *Engineering Quality by Design* (1990); J. L. Bossert, *Quality Function Deployment: A Practitioner's Approach* (1990); and R. C. Camp, *Benchmarking: The Search for Industry Best Practices that Lead to Superior Performance* (1989).
3. For a more complete discussion of this subject, refer to J. Campanella (ed.), *Principles of Quality Costs, Second Edition, Principles, Implementation and Use,* (ASQC Quality Costs Committee, Quality Press, 1990).

CHAPTER 3

The Critical Role of Human Relations

1. Material in this chapter is excerpted from *BBP Handbook of Quality Management*, 1992. Copyrighted material reprinted with permission of BBP HANDBOOK OF QUALITY MANAGEMENT and Bureau of Business Practice, 24 Rope Ferry Road, Waterford, CT 06386.
2. Material in "Common Pitfalls for Management" is excerpted by permission from R. A. Dumas, "Organizationwide Quality: How to Avoid Common Pitfalls," *Quality Progress,* May 1989, pp. 41–44.
3. Material in "The Crucial Role of People" is excerpted by permission from K. Bemowski, "People: The Only Thing That Will Make Quality Work," *Quality Progress,* September 1988, pp. 63–67.
4. Material in "Resolving Human Relations Conflicts" is excerpted by permission from D. K. Denton, "Four Steps to Resolving Conflicts," *Quality Progress,* April 1989, pp. 29–33.
5. For a more complete discussion of this subject, refer to the following Quality Press books: J. P. Kern, J. J. Riley, and L. N. Jones (eds.), *Human Resources Management* (ASQC Human Resources Division, 1987); R. J. Pierce, *Involvement Engineering: Engaging*

Employees in Quality and Productivity (1986); and S. P. Rubinstein, *Participative Systems at Work: Creating Quality and Employment Security* (1987).

CHAPTER 4

Quality Improvement Approaches in the Service Sector

1. Material in this chapter is excerpted from *BBP Handbook of Quality Management,* 1992. Copyrighted material reprinted with permission of BBP HANDBOOK OF QUALITY MANAGEMENT and Bureau of Business Practice, 24 Rope Ferry Road, Waterford, CT 06386.
2. Material in this subsection (two paragraphs) is excerpted by permission from *Service America.* K. Albrecht and R. Zemke (Homewood, Ill.: Richard D. Irwin, Inc., 1985), p.32.
3. Material in this subsection (five paragraphs) is excerpted by permission from C. A. King, "Service Quality Assurance Is Different, *Quality Progress,* June 1985, pp. 14–18.
4. Material in "Defining Quality in Service Businesses" is excerpted from M. B. Brown, "Defining Quality in Service Businesses," and reprinted with permission from QUALITY (January 1988, pp. 56–58), a publication of Hitchcock Publishing, a Capital Cities/ABC, Inc., Company.
5. Material in "A Quality Strategy for Service Organizations" is excerpted by permission from R. W. Butterfield, "A Quality Strategy for Service Organizations," *Quality Progress,* December 1987, pp. 40–42.
6. Material in "Quality Planning for Service Industries" is excerpted by permission from R. N. Kacker, "Quality Planning for Service Industries," *Quality Progress,* August 1988, pp. 39–42.
7. Material in "Creating a Customer-Centered Culture for Service Quality" is excerpted by permission from R. Lawton, "Creating a Customer-Centered Culture for Service Quality," *Quality Progress,* May 1989, pp. 34–36. © Robin Lawton, Innovative Management Technologies, Inc., Minneapolis, 1989. Reprinted by permission.
8. Material in "Quality Plan Development: A Step toward Customer Enthusiasm" is excerpted by permission from J. S. Sarazen, "Quality Plan Development: A Key Step toward Customer Enthusiasm," *Quality Progress,* October 1988, pp. 72–75.
9. For a more complete discussion of this subject, refer to the following Quality Press books: R. W. Butterfield, *Quality Service—Pure and Simple* (1990); W. F. Drewes, *Quality Dynamics for the Service Industry* (1991); and H. L. Lefevre, *Quality Service Pays* (1989).

CHAPTER 5

Total Quality Management—The Ultimate Adage for Quality

1. Material in this chapter was adapted from *Total Quality Management Guide—A Two Volume Guide for Defense Organizations, Volume I—Key Features of the DOD Implementation,* a publication of the U.S. Department of Defense (final draft, February 2, 1990).

CHAPTER 6

The Central Idea of Quality Improvement

1. For a more complete discussion of the subject, refer to the following Quality Press books: H. D. Shuster, *Teaming for Quality Improvement* (1990); and C. A. Aubrey and P. K. Felkins, *Teamwork: Involving People in Quality and Productivity Improvement* (1988).

CHAPTER 7

Personal Guidelines for the Journey

1. Material in this chapter was adapted from *Total Quality Management Guide—A Two Volume Guide for Defense Organizations, Volume II—A Guide to Implementation*, a publication of the U.S. Department of Defense (final draft, February 15, 1990). It is excerpted from copyrighted material with permission of BBP HANDBOOK OF QUALITY MANAGEMENT and Bureau of Business Practice, 24 Rope Ferry Road, Waterford, CT 06386.

INDEX

Other books of interest to you from Business One Irwin . . .

GLOBAL QUALITY
A Synthesis of the World's Best Management Methods
Richard Tabor Greene
Co-published with ASQC Quality Press

Finally, a book that organizes the chaos of quality improvement techniques! Greene compiles 24 global quality systems and the 30 characteristics they share, plus 8 new business systems, into this convenient reference. Also reveals seven new quality improvement techniques being tested in Japan! (884 pages)
ISBN: 1-55623-915-7

QUALITY IN AMERICA
How to Implement a Competitive Quality Program
V. Daniel Hunt
Co-published with ASQC Quality Press

Dramatically improve your firm's market share, performance, and profitability! Hunt, the author of several award-winning productivity improvement books, analyzes the present state of the practice of quality in America and helps you understand the theories, basic tools, and techniques that can improve quality in your organization. (308 pages)
ISBN: 1-55623-536-4

THE CORPORATE GUIDE TO THE MALCOLM BALDRIDGE NATIONAL QUALITY AWARD
Proven Strategies for Building Quality into Your Organization
New and Revised
Marion Mills Steeples
Co-published with ASQC Quality Press

Foreword by Robert W. Galvin,
Chairman of the Executive Committee, Motorola, Inc.

The insider's guide to the coveted quality award! Marion Steeples—a member of the Baldridge Board of Examiners since the award's inception—explains the major categories and their requirements; lessons learned from the winning companies; and how your organization can cut costs, streamline processes, and enhance worker morale. (358 pages)
ISBN: 1-55623-957-2